Standing Ground

ALSO BY ALAN L. WHITE

Alaska Behind Blue Eyes

Alaska Stories, Police Tales, and
Things I'd Rather Not Talk About

Standing Ground

Alan L. White

Dark River

Clare, Michigan

Published by DARK RIVER
P.O. Box 436
Clare, Michigan 48617

Publisher's Cataloging-in-Publication Data
White, Alan L.
    Standing Ground: Alaska stories, police tales, and things I'd rather not talk
    about / Alan L. White — Clare, MI.: Dark River, 2001.
        p.   cm.
    ISBN 0-9663201-0-7
    ISBN 0-9663201-1-5 (pbk.)

    1. Police—Fiction. 2. Hunting—Fiction. 3. Fishing—Fiction.
    4. Alaska—Fiction. 5. Adventure fiction. I. Title.
PS3573.H45 A15   2001   2001-88416
813.54—dc21   CIP

Project Coordination by Jenkins Group Inc. • www.bookpublishing.com

Cover photo of Mark Todd on Dewey Mountain taken by the author.

05 04 03 02 01 ∿ 5 4 3 2 1

Printed in the United States of America

This book is dedicated to the memory of
Benjamin Matthew White,
who loved balloons.

1996-1999

CONTENTS

SPECIAL THANKS

FIRST AND FOREMOST I WOULD LIKE THANK MY FAVORITE HIGH school teacher and good friend Lynn Laskowski for his editorial guidance and kind support of this project. It took twenty years but Lynn got through to me. I am glad he never gave up.

I would also like to thank Jamie LaPoe for her help and bubbling enthusiasm for my writing.

Special thanks also to my current and former D.A.R.E. kids for teaching me more than they will ever know.

Many thanks to Ken White who always seems to believe in the big guy.

Credit goes to Mark Todd for pushing me when needed, even up the mountains of Alaska.

To Larry Everts for his continuing love and firm support.

I would also like to thank my mom and dad for believing in their son.

I am indebted to Chief Tim Rynearson of the Clare City Police for his patience and support of an officer who likes to write stories.

And, of course, thanks goes to my wife, Nettie; and our children, Jon and Jennifer, for putting up with me.

INTRODUCTION

NEW AUTHORS ARE ANXIOUS. WELL, PERHAPS NEUROTIC WOULD be a better word. After I finished my first book I spent countless hours planning its release—down to the most annoying detail—then I spent more time worrying about the detail. I kind of felt like a five-year-old getting on a school bus for the first time; I was proud of what I had accomplished, but afraid of the many challenges to come. Although I was ready for my first book to face the world, I was extremely anxious about how the world would receive it.

Being a new author is also like being a new parent, in that I talked endlessly about my first book. This was easy in my hometown, somewhat easy in nearby cities—but the difficulty definitely increased proportionately the further I traveled from central Michigan. Throughout the first year of promoting *Alaska Behind Blue Eyes*, I signed books in stores that ranged from national chains to small independent outlets. I presented programs to audiences, large and small, all over Michigan and in other states. However, it was the media interviews that brought the most challenge.

Although I am someone who loves to talk, I was not always comfortable with the press. I gave interviews to small venues mostly, the kind of newspapers, radio, and television stations that concentrate on students-of-the-month far more than national news. You know, the media that enjoy reporting a story about a small-town cop who likes to write stories. Except one day—a reporter from a large metropolitan newspaper contacted me.

At first I could not believe that this paper was interested in *Alaska Behind Blue Eyes*. Far away from Clare, a newspaper reporter from a southern Michigan city with a six-figure population and a ten-figure skyline, asked me for an interview. Of course I was excited—and neurotic—about the idea. The publicity from the resulting article would be wonderful, *if* I did not mess it up.

I drove nearly two hours south of Clare and met with the reporter, who was younger than me, in a room far older than both of us combined. I did my best to sound like I knew what I was doing.

Actually, the interview went quite well. Most of the questions he asked were similar to the ones already asked of me in small towns and I began to feel confident—until he posed his last question. "So tell me, Officer White," he asked with a smile, "how would you describe your writing style?"

"My writing style?" I repeated slowly, trying to stall.

"Yes, Officer White, your style of writing. What would you compare it with?"

"A bowl of Chex Party Mix," I answered.

My interviewer looked up from his yellow legal pad with a confused expression. "Chex Mix?" he queried slowly.

"Yeah, you know, baked Chex cereal, pretzels, seasonings . . ."

"I am familiar with the product, Officer White. I'm just not sure of the correlation with a writing style."

I took a deep breath. "I don't write fine literature. Heck, I don't even write thick literature. I don't try to compare myself with the great masters of the writing world. I cannot write like Tolstoy, Faulkner, or even Hemingway. But, who wants to read Tolstoy all the time? It would be like dressing up and sitting down to a literary Thanksgiving dinner three times a day. Sometimes people just like to put on an old pair of faded jeans, a torn sweatshirt and munch on a heaping bowl of wordy Chex Mix. It's fun. I don't try to change the world with my writing. I try to write stories that people like to read in the bathroom or on a rainy Sunday afternoon."

"Officer White," the reporter said as he closed his notebook. "I am shocked."

"Because you don't like the Chex Mix metaphor?" I asked.

"No, Officer White. I am shocked because I actually understand the Chex thing."

In *Standing Ground* that is what you, the reader, will get; a big bowl of snack words from an ordinary man in a not so ordinary job who likes to write about ordinary things in a not so ordinary way. You will read about other experiences I had while working in Skagway, Alaska as a police officer that I did not include in *Alaska Behind Blue Eyes*. Some essays are based on my experiences as an officer in Clare, Michigan. Yet others will tell of fishing and hunting adventures, household problems, and even about an incident when I worked as a paramedic.

These are individual stories without a central theme. *Standing Ground* is a collection of thoughts that became a bowl of flavors, both funny and sad, that hopefully will satisfy you on a rainy day or even in the bathroom. And, like Chex Mix, I hope you are left wanting for more.

Standing Ground

INITIATIONS

WE ALL REMEMBER OUR FIRST TIME. IT FEELS LIKE ACCOMplishing a lifetime goal, the one thing that we have fantasized about and rehearsed in our heads to the point of obsession. Countless hours in the back of classrooms and before the glowing lights of dashboards are spent fantasizing about this turning point from youthful dream to adult reality. And then, one night, it happens. We are so nervous that we cannot decide which is worse, the trembling hands, the pounding heart, or the cold sweat that seems to seep from every pore. Nevertheless, it is important to remember that we all make it through this initial event and look back fondly on the experience, no matter how *inexperienced* we were. After all, a police officer's first arrest is something that he or she will never forget.

My first arrest came on the second shift I worked alone. With a grand total of eleven hours of police seasoning, I stopped a car for erratic driving on Clare's McEwan Street. (For those who lack knowledge in basic police terminology, "erratic driving" simply means the car was being driven in the far right lane, and the inside lane, and in the two oncoming lanes, and occasionally bouncing off the curbs.) Luckily the wee morning hours in Clare held little traffic. I turned on my patrol unit's emergency beacons, sometimes referred to as the disco lights, and made my first solo traffic stop.

It was difficult to call in my location to dispatch since my hand gripped the microphone with enough force to crack a walnut shell and my mouth was as dry as central Arizona. It was also difficult to leave my patrol unit without first unbuckling my safety belt, as I found out after several unsuccessful attempts. Finally, I did make it to the driver's door of the car, although it was somewhat embarrassing to stand next to a strange vehicle, that moments before was using city curbs as guardrails, while my knees shook enough to make Elvis jealous. By the time I had the guy out of the car, I was ready to call time-out and take a break.

He was drunk, that was certain. I managed to stumble through the field sobriety tests confirming this fact. Then came the moment I had been waiting for my entire life. I was about to say the words that would make me a real police officer. Things would be different from this point, since I would no longer be a police virgin.

"You are under arrest," I commanded. Actually, it came out more like a suggestion. Some might even call it a question, judging by the drunk's reaction.

"You sure?" he asked, looking at me with bloodshot eyes.

"Yes!"

"You feeling all right, officer? You don't look so good."

"You are under arrest for drunk driving! Now, turn around and put your hands behind your back," I offered.

He did as I **suggested** and waited patiently as I pulled out my handcuffs. I took this opportunity to break into a cold sweat and to drop the cuffs on the pavement, where they skidded under his car.

"You want me to get those for you?" he asked.

"No."

"Is there anything I can do to help, officer?" he asked. "I mean, it seems that I have a lot more experience getting drunk than you do arresting people."

"I know what I'm doing," I stated, unsure of whom I was trying to convince.

By the time the guy was cuffed, searched, and seated in my patrol unit, I was a wreck.

My hands were shaking as I tried to write the required information in my daily log. Attempting to look and act like a seasoned veteran wasn't easy. Even though I had just made my first arrest, I still felt like a little kid working undercover in a grown-up world. For one thing, my appearance was not exactly that of a veteran. At twenty years old, not only did I have a boyish face, I was not even shaving my face every day. This realization was compounded by the grinning man sitting uncomfortably shackled in the backseat.

"Officer," he said, changing expression from mirth to concern. "Do you mind if I ask you a personal question?"

"Go ahead," I replied, pretending to write on my pad.

"Does your momma know you're out this late?"

One of the best first-arrest stories came from Rich, a young officer who began his police career in Clare. Although Rich is now a fairly distinguished-looking Michigan state trooper, I remember when he could have been voted most likely to faint under pressure. He looked so young that we used to joke with him about working Halloween foot patrol and getting more candy from homeowners than the local children.

Rich's first arrest was a drunk driver that he had stopped on a particularly hot and still spring night. Being a young—but very well-trained officer—Rich positioned his patrol unit about fifteen feet behind the drunk's vehicle. The problem was that also sharing this fifteen feet of space was a long-dead and profusely bloated carcass of a road-kill white-tailed deer. Rich nearly gagged when he walked past the rotting body and approached the driver's side of the car. The driver was obviously intoxicated and could not be asked to move his vehicle again.

Being a rookie, Rich conducted his investigation between the cars, next to Bambi's slowly liquefying mother. I only wish that I could have watched as he explained the field sobriety test, while swatting the swarming flies. I believe the drunk's last words before being arrested were: "Whew! Is that me or you, officer?"

WAITING FOR LOVE

H E CAME EVERY MORNING. WELL, ALMOST EVERY MORNING. Sometimes, if the rain was very hard or if the temperature fell well below zero, he would not come, but every other day he was there with his brown coat and two dog leashes in his left hand. I could look out my window at exactly seven o'clock and watch as he walked to the heavy oak door. Four knocks. Never more and never less. It must have been their code. She was always ready, too. He never had to wait more than a few seconds. She would smile and take his hand and walk with him down my street. From my living room window in my tiny Alaskan home I was privileged to watch two people in love.

Her name was Violet. It was an easy name to remember because she planted dozens of the flowers in front of her house and along the front walk. During the long days of the Alaskan summer, the purple and pink blossoms turned the large white house into a showplace of beauty. She lived by herself, although I would never consider her alone based on the amount of people who came and went throughout the day. Children came in the late mornings and afternoons, some happy and some sad, but all were prepared for their piano lessons. Violet insisted that they come prepared. In the evenings it was the people from her church. Violet was very active in her church and most of the Bible study meetings and choir practices took place in the large white house with all the flowers.

I think she was in her late seventies. Gray-streaked black hair crowned her head over an always joyful face. I was told that Violet had worked for over forty years for the railroad before retiring years ago. To most of the community, however, she was known as the piano lady.

William, the man who called on Violet each morning, was known as Willy to the members of this Alaskan town. He was born in Skagway and worked for the Park Service for nearly as long as Violet worked for the rails. Willy was gaining ground on eighty, but his youthful gait and smiling face made him look much younger. He was known in our community as the person to call for any task involving welding. In his garage was a large collection of welding supplies and Willy was always eager to repair anything made of metal that unintentionally came apart. Oftentimes I would walk by his neat brown house and see him in the garage, a welding helmet over his face while a thankful citizen waited patiently as hot sparks flew. Not surprisingly, Willy had a fine display of violets under each of his front windows.

Willy was also active in the community. Over his years in Alaska, he had served several times on the city council and on many different boards. He was a member of our local Lions Club and was always put in charge of fundraising because of his pleasant demeanor. If Willy came to your door selling raffle tickets or soliciting money, you could not say no.

I have no idea when Willy began meeting Violet for their morning walks. I asked several locals and no one could say except it was as long ago as they could remember. They referred to their walks as a public service, but I and the rest of the community knew it was because they enjoyed each others company.

Each morning Willy would knock for Violet, and they would walk other people's dogs. They would each carry a leash, pick up dogs that were chained outside, walk them around a couple blocks, and return them home. They did this for several hours each day. As far as I knew, Violet and Willy never asked permission, mainly because none was needed in a town like Skagway. Each day while on patrol I would see the happy couple holding hands while two dogs playfully pulled along from opposite sides. The hopeless romantic in me could see the love between them and began to wonder why they were only together in the mornings and not the rest of the day. It took the rear bumper nearly falling off my truck to help me understand.

Never forgetting my landscaping roots, I was helping a friend pull out some stumps for a rather elaborate shrub planting project. The combination of a heavy logging chain and a stubborn juniper stump caused the aging bumper on my battered truck to give way long before the deep tap root of the evergreen. This resulted in my bumper sagging from my truck like a depressing frown.

The following day I was backed into Willy's garage while he surveyed the damage.

"Well, Officer White," Willy said with his always upbeat voice. "It seems you have answered the time honored question of what happens when an immovable object meets an irresistible force." He looked at me over his glasses like my high school shop teacher, then ran his hand over the downturned bumper. "Something's got to give."

"Can you fix it, Willy?" I asked, knowing the answer.

"I can fix anything, Officer White. You know that."

He removed the bumper and used a sledgehammer to make it almost straight. Then he welded a new bracket to my truck frame and drilled some holes for the new bolts. Within an hour my truck was repaired. Willy put away his tools and grabbed a couple of diet sodas from his garage refrigerator. I took a long swig and decided to pry a little. "Say, Willy," I said, turning the can over in my hands and pretending to read the small print on the label. "You know that I live across the street from Violet."

Willy's face became concerned and he slammed down his soda can, grabbing his chest with his right hand. "You do? So that's why a Skagway police car sits in the road all the time. All these months I thought Violet was living next door to felons." He stopped faking a heart attack and laughed out loud, looking at me over his glasses. "Everyone in town knows where you live, Al." Willy picked up his soda and took a long drink. "What's on your mind young man?"

I turned the can around a couple more times then took a sip. "Every morning I see you two walking the dogs."

"Someone's got to walk the dogs," he said. "Most of the poor things are chained up all day." Willy set his can down and leaned against the workbench.

"You seem to get along so well."

Willy smiled softly, obviously enjoying my questioning. "Violet is a wonderful woman. I don't know what I would do without her."

"Look, Willy," I said. "It's none of my business and I'm a little embarrassed to ask, but since you are both alone and not getting any younger, why don't you guys get married? You two look great together. Everyone in town says you have been seeing each other for as long as they can remember."

Willy smiled and looked down, kicking at an oxygen hose from a green tank. "Officer White, you are right on three counts. First, it *is* none of your business. Second, we *are* both alone. Finally, *none of us* is getting any younger." He looked up and adjusted his glasses, never losing his smile.

"I'm sorry. I didn't mean to pry."

"Sure you did, Al. But that's okay. I don't mind talking about Violet. The truth is I have asked her to marry me many times. Every Christmas Eve and every Valentine's Day. Unfortunately, she always says no." Willy picked up the hose from the floor and wrapped it around the top of the tank.

"That's too bad, Willy," I said, hoping he really didn't mind the questioning. "How long have you been seeing each other?"

"In terms of months or years?"

"Years, I guess."

"Thirty-seven."

I nearly dropped the can of soda in mid-drink. "Did you say *thirty-seven?*"

"Yes, Al. Thirty-seven years this October."

"That's before I was born!"

Willy smiled and wheeled the tank to the side of the garage. He grabbed a rag and wiped his hands slowly. "It has been a long time," he said.

"Look, Willy," I said, trying to pick my words carefully. "After *thirty-seven* years of pursuing the same woman who refuses to marry you, don't you think it may be time to date someone else?"

Willy leaned against the workbench and folded his arms across his chest. An expression of determination came over his face as he looked at me. "No, Al," he said. "There is no one else for me. Besides, I think that I am beginning to wear her down."

WOODSTOCK

WOODSTOCK WAS BORN IN JUNE, WHEN THE SPIREA BUSHES stood bent over from the weight of countless white blossoms and looking as if they were caught in a freak snowfall. It was 1984. I had just graduated from the police academy at Delta College. I remember that I never felt more confident in myself or in what direction my life would take. I would be a police officer and a good one. Period. As the confusion of my life's previous misdirection faded in that warm spring, I finally understood what it meant to be a man and what it meant to understand life. I wish that I could feel that way again.

Because I was still working part-time that summer, I supplemented my income by working for some of my old landscaping accounts. Most of my time was spent trimming trees and planting gardens for Bob, my favorite customer. Bob was old enough to be my grandfather, if not my great-grandfather, and he had a way of making everything he said sound important. Bob was a gentleman of impeccable taste and shared my love of hunting waterfowl and upland birds.

A giant golden retriever, that he talked of reverently, was always by his side. It wasn't long before I developed a love for the breed. I made plans to own one, for many reasons, but mainly because I wished to be like Bob. Bob was someone that a young man could use as a role model.

Early that spring I ordered a puppy from a reputable kennel downstate, long before his mother was bred to a champion sire. As Bob had suggested, I took no chances in the breeding. Any listing of golden retriever field-trial champions contained nearly all of their ancestors, giving them bloodlines that went back, almost, to Noah's Ark. On paper he had the makings of a true champion.

I brought Woodstock home when he was eight weeks old and nothing more than a ball of golden-red energy with huge feet. Because he would run across the yard with glee, only to tumble over his oversized feet, I named him Woodstock, after the Peanuts yellow cartoon bird. From the beginning he showed signs of greatness.

Before he was even comfortable with his name, Woody, as I called him, would bring me things. Lots of things. I would take him out for a romp in the yard and watch, amazed as he picked up twigs, leaves, rocks, and anything else that he could fit into his small mouth and bring to me. He was a natural. By the time Woody was twelve weeks old he was making nearly perfect retrieves with a training dummy. Already I could picture him sitting alongside me in the duck blind, waiting to retrieve downed birds. A dog like Woody could find a duck in the thickest cattails or a grouse in the deepest tangles.

That fall he was still too young to hunt with me, but I continued with his training. By the time the snow was too deep to work in, Woody was making triple blind retrieves. That is: I would hide three dummies in different types of cover up to a hundred yards away. I could bring him out and by hand signals alone, he could retrieve each to my hand. My friends were amazed at his talent and even more amazed that it was I who had taught him.

That first winter is when I began to notice that Woody had a few strange quirks. For instance, he liked to put things *in* things. As if to entertain me, he would drag some type of container, a shoe box, a laundry basket, a boot, etc., into the living room and then fill it with socks, balls, or any small, loose items laying around the house. He also did this during the night while I was sleeping. Many mornings I would put on my boots, only to find they contained a tennis ball or an old rag. As amusing as these antics were, this was but one of his several odd traits.

For reasons only known to a golden retriever with an Ivy League pedigree, Woody also liked to shut himself or others in rooms. He would enter a room and shut the door from the inside, then bark to be let out. This happened so often that I began closing the doors, or propping them open, rather than getting up to let him out two or three times an hour. For doors that closed the other way, he would wait until I was busy doing something in a room and swing the door shut from the outside, then bark to be let in. I began to think that either he was dumb as a ball of twine or so intelligent that I could not understand him. I still don't know.

No matter how much wisdom flowed through his brain, one thing that Woody could do was read my thoughts. It started late that first winter when he began to grow large and lose some of his puppy playfulness. I would come home from a busy and mentally draining day at the police department and sit in my favorite chair, hoping to relax. Woody would come to me, put his head in my lap and look up at me with those dark-brown eyes. His expression was one of concern, along with a little confusion as to why I was so tense. He seemed to be analyzing my mood, studying my anxiousness. I would rub his ears and pat his head halfheartedly with my thoughts still on police work. Woody would react to this by running in circles and chasing his tail. Every minute or so, he would stop to see if I was watching him and if I was still bothered by things over which I had no control. After a few minutes I would laugh and say "All right" and he would come to me again and rest his head in my lap with a look of satisfaction.

Woody slept in my bed, lying close to my body and listening to the sounds of the house, as if he was protecting me from the darkness. In the mornings he would put his paws on my chest and lick my face to let me know the scary night was over and he was there for me. All day he followed me, watching with an alertness I had never seen in a dog. I never felt more protected than when Woody was by my side.

When spring came I polished his retriever training to perfection. One day I picked up a road-killed grouse and took it home for his introduction to birds. He sniffed the bird with interest, carefully investigating the feathered thing. Calling him to heel, I tossed the grouse far out on the green grass then gave him the command. Woody shot away from me with great speed and reached the bird in seconds. As he slid to a stop, I could sense his confusion as he looked at the bird and then to me. After a short pause, Woody left the grouse and returned slowly to my side. He seemed embarrassed. He looked around for the training dummy. Again I gave him the command and again he ran to the bird, only to return with an empty mouth. *This cannot be happening,* I thought. *I have the perfect dog, an animal that was bred for retrieving birds and who shows so much promise.*

I worked with Woody for an hour. Gently I tried everything from offers of treats to putting the bird into his mouth and talking to him softly. Nothing worked. We went inside and Woody moped around, hanging his head apologetically. I thought that it was just a bad day and tomorrow would be different. It wasn't.

In the coming months I consulted every retriever owner I knew, and several that I did not. We traveled hours from home, meeting with breeders and hunters, and even an animal psychologist. Really. I read books and magazines, looking for an answer to Woody's problem with feathered things. Finally, I took him to Bob. I was very embarrassed, but I asked for help. Bob worked with Woody for days, and spent hours in his yard before he told me that I had a fine dog that would make a wonderful companion—but not a bird retriever. He said that I should resign myself to the fact that I had a terrific dog that would pick up anything—as long as it had never once been alive.

Giving Woody away never occurred to me. Woody was such a big part of my life that he would be mine forever—bird retriever or not. I always took him hunting with me, although this presented several embarrassing moments on the marsh and in the woods. I would sit in a duck blind and knock a duck down, only to row to the downed bird with Woody leading the way from the front of the boat. Hunting for upland game was a little different. Most bird-hunting dogs smell the scent of a grouse, woodcock, or any other game, and get excited. But Woody would get worried. I would stalk through the forest and watch him for signs of anxiety, then head in the direction he avoided. It was a difficult system to master, but it worked.

For the past several years I have fed ducks along the river in my backyard. After putting out several pounds of corn on the bank, I can enjoy up to a hundred mallards flying in to feed. If my Labrador, Taku, is out, the ducks wait in the river. If Woody is in the yard they will come in and feed, while my prized golden retriever barks at the back door to be let in. I don't know what is more embarrassing; the fact that Woody is scared of the birds or the fact that the ducks some-how know of his fear and feed in my yard only twenty feet from a seventy-pound dog that was bred to retrieve them.

Ever since that summer of 1984, Woody has been my constant companion. He is always there for me and always senses my thoughts and makes me feel important to him. I could not have hoped for a better friend. He has seen me though several girlfriends, several breakups, and nine years of marriage. All during this time I never imagined what it would be like without him in my life. I still can't.

Woody turned sixteen this spring. No one I know has ever had a dog this long, especially one of Woody's breed. He sleeps a lot and no longer has the control over himself he had when he was younger, although this is to be expected. But Woody still likes to walk with me, and he enjoys looking at the river. I constantly hope for a few more years that I know will never come.

Woody still sleeps with me, but on the floor next to my bed because his legs no longer allow him to jump up on things. Sometimes he gets scared at night. I will wake to find him by the bed with a worried expression when he hears a strange noise or when he wants to be by my side and cannot. I reach my hand down to rub his ears and pat his head. I tell him that everything is fine, but I still worry about him. I share his worry and want to take him back to that summer of 1984, when the world was mine and we were both young and sure of what life was and could be.

Woody passed away quietly in my arms shortly before the publication of this book.

CALIFORNIA DREAMING

S TEVE GRIPPED THE HANDLEBARS TIGHTLY THROUGH HIS BLACK leather gloves. He accelerated quickly and felt the bike respond confidently under him. He shifted into a higher gear and leaned on the next curve, enjoying the G-forces as they pulled at his belly.

The road was still black from a recent rain, but now that the sun had appeared, the road was clearing of puddles and the ocean had turned to a golden, frothy surf. The guardrail running along the coastal highway was the only barrier separating the road from the Pacific Ocean and the mountains of northern California.

The motorcycle under Steve was a custom Harley, black as night and so powerful it sometimes scared him. He could feel the power through the seat, while his ears drank in the sound only a well-tuned Harley can make. It sounded like hunger. Steve looked out over the sea, then to the road ahead; a road that extended onward forever.

The angry honking of the car behind him brought Steve back to reality. Removed from the California coast, Steve was now alert in Clare, Michigan, stopped dead in his van before a green traffic light at the city's main intersection. He tried to move through the light, but it changed before he could reach the intersection. Steve stopped again and leaned out the window. I watched him from the opposite side of the road.

If a picture says a thousand words, this image of Steve, at the intersection of Fifth and McEwan in Clare, says many more.

For reasons only known to me, I sometimes see people in situations that stay in my mind like snapshots. These images are stored in my memory where I work on them until a story unfolds. I worked a great deal on the image of Steve.

With the light now red, Steve leaned out the window of his new gold minivan, his elbow fully outside the vehicle and his head halfway out the window, sagging in a look of surrender. The van was new, of this I was sure, because of the dealership sticker still visible on the back window. On the front passenger seat a boy of about five frolicked. Behind the boy, strapped in a car seat, was a girl of about three. She was teasing the boy in front of her by pulling on his hair. Across from the girl was an infant in a child seat, crying and flailing its arms. Blocking the sun from the infant was a Winnie-the-Pooh sun screen.

I guessed Steve was in his mid-thirties. He probably had a well-paying job and a moderate mortgage. His wife would have been attending a civic function or working an odd shift, leaving Steve responsible for the children. Responsible. That is what Steve is now; a responsible man in a small town in a gold minivan stuck under a stoplight.

It wasn't always this way. Twenty years before, Steve would have been an important member of his high school's football team, running over the groomed grass of the field each Friday night to the roar of the hometown crowd and impressing the head cheerleader. His life then was without responsibility, devoid of children, mortgages, and minivans. Summer nights were spent with his friends, drinking beer, looking at the stars over a woodland campfire, and planning adventure.

But youthful dreams that seemed so important twenty years ago led to a college education and back to the cheerleader and the gold minivan that held his children under the stoplight.

It's not that Steve resented his life. Not at all. In fact, he enjoyed the comfort and security of marriage and a loving wife. But the joy of family and a secure job still did not obscure the visions of youthful splendor. Sometimes Steve needed to return there, if only for a minute, away from his squirming children and the red traffic light. At these times he was back on the Harley, riding up the wet blackness of the Pacific Coast highway, looking over the gold ocean that, oh so much, matched the color of his minivan.

BEYOND THE CALL

A POLICE OFFICER IN A SMALL TOWN HAS MANY DUTIES ABOVE and beyond what would normally be considered *law enforcement*. For instance, in Clare the local police are responsible for maintaining the amount of water that flows over Shamrock Dam. They watch for lighted alarms that signal a broken sewer lift station, report burned out mercury lights, deliver letters to local officials, unlock car and house doors, and respond to all ambulance calls. The reason for this extra service is that small towns often lack the resources of larger cities.

I really don't mind these extra jobs. After all, I entered police service because I liked to help people, even if this meant standing in the pouring rain on a dark night while raising the heavy boards of our city dam. One morning, however, changed my way of thinking about civic duty.

It was one of those winter mornings when the roads were slick with freezing rain and the populace at large had forgotten how to drive without the benefit of traction. Our ambulance and fire crews had been busy most of the night out on the expressway, taking care of injured people from many car accidents. They were still dealing with the last few accidents several miles from town when a call came in. An ambulance was needed at a local apartment complex for an unknown medical call. Unknown medical calls are common when the person requesting the ambulance has someone else call, who in turn has someone else call, followed by asking someone else to call, etc.

I was near the building when the call came in. I knew would be alone for quite awhile before the ambulance crew could clear their accident. These types of things happen sometimes, normally I just talk to the people and try to keep them calm until the *real* medical help arrives. So, it was with relative calm that I climbed the steps and knocked on the apartment door. A female voice called out for me to enter. Actually, it screamed, "Get in here!" Something in the tone of the voice made me think this could be my most memorable call.

As I walked across the brown shag carpet, slowing slightly because I was not sure if I really wanted to see what lay behind door number one, I could hear crying in the back bedroom. A woman screeched again, as my trembling hand touched the knob. The door swung open with a high-pitched whine that did nothing to cover the sobbing person on the bed.

Her hair was matted to her forehead with sweat, and her eyes were red from crying. Long dark hair lay on her shoulders, touching her small pink nightgown and barely covering her huge distended abdomen. My thoughts flashed back to our town's only paramedics working on accident victims out on the highway and then to the way the woman held her belly. My first reaction to finding myself in this particular apartment could best be described by the word, DAMN. My moment of hesitation was not lost on the woman.

"Hurry! The baby's coming!" she screamed.

I took a deep breath and pulled out my best officer voice. "You'll have to wait. The ambulance will be here in awhile."

The woman raised her head off the pillow and gave me a look that dropped the temperature in the room nearly twenty degrees. "I *said*, the baby's coming!" Her face contorted gruesomely and I expected sparks to fly from her eyes at any moment. She now resembled the girl from the movie *The Exorcist*. "Check to see if I'm crowning!" she screamed.

Crowning. I wasn't sure what she meant at first, then I remembered the film I saw years ago in the police academy when we were taught how to deliver a baby. The academy instructors thought it was important for all officers to be able to assist in a birth should medical personnel not be present. I remember thinking at the time how stupid this was. Now, standing in a suddenly cold room with a very pregnant woman who was screaming for me to check her, I wished I had paid more attention to that particular class.

Crowning, I thought again. *Oh yeah. That is when the baby's head starts to show from the . . . well, show.* "Just try to remain calm," I said gently.

"Get over here!" she yelled, holding onto her knees to brace against the next contraction.

"What's your name?" I asked, thinking that under the circumstances we may as well be acquainted.

"Anne!" she cried out.

I walked slowly to the foot of the bed and looked under her nightgown. My hands were shaking and my heart was pounding. Anne was, indeed, crowning.

"Well!" she yelled.

"You're going to have a baby very soon."

"No kidding!" she screamed, like it was my fault, as she suffered though another contraction.

She *was* going to have a baby. Right here. Right now. This fact I knew for certain as I could see part of the baby's head. At this moment I found myself in a state of disbelief. This shouldn't happen.

There should be paramedics here. There should be someone here who had at least once delivered a baby. I kept thinking that at any moment a doctor would walk through the door and tell me to stand aside. I kept thinking that I should call someone. Then I realized that she had called for help—and instead had gotten me.

I ran to the bathroom and found a pile of clean towels. I returned to the bed and put a large towel underneath her. She cried out again and I saw the baby's head advance a little. "Push!" I yelled, hoping it was the right command. Anne was tired, frustrated, and angry, but she knew how to push. My eyes grew wide as the baby's head moved further. I could see tiny veins and even some dark hair on its head. She pushed again and the head came halfway out. The baby's tiny nose and mouth pointed downward toward the towel. With another push the entire head was out and, to my relief, the baby started to cry. I told her to push again, but the baby seemed stuck. Somehow I remembered one part of my academy movie. I reached in and pushed one of the baby's shoulders down while pulling gently on its head. With a pop the shoulder came out. I repeated the procedure with the other side and the baby began to move.

The baby was now crying, loudly. I was happy about that, but I was thinking about something else. I remembered my mother telling me what a beautiful thing childbirth was. Right. Until you see it up close. I hate to disappoint anyone who is waiting for this event, but the baby looked like a slimy blue-green lizard trying desperately to crawl from a tight space. At this point it didn't even look human. It looked more like a creature from the movie *Alien*.

Anne was crying, the baby was crying, and I was a shaking wreck. The baby was being born before my watering eyes. One more push and the baby kind of slipped out. I turned it over and used another towel to wipe some of the slime off. Suddenly the baby began to change color. It went from the color of pond scum to almost pink in a matter of seconds. *Cool.* The umbilical cord was resting over my hand. I could feel it pulse with the strong beating of Anne's heart. She sat up slightly and looked down at her baby.

"Is it a boy or girl?" she asked.

"You have a son," I said, wrapping the baby in a towel and laying it on her belly. She reached down and held it gently, rubbing her hand over the soft head.

"Thank you," she said quietly.

"Oh, that's okay," I said. "I didn't have much else to do today."

Anne laughed through her tears and look lovingly at her son. "What's your name?" she asked.

Suddenly I was excited. She was going to name her son after me. What an honor. What a wonderful thing to tell my friends. A lasting tribute to a heroic act. Well, at least a scared-to-death act. "My name is Alan," I said proudly.

"Oh," she said quietly. "What's your middle name?"

"Lloyd."

"Oh." She looked at my face and smiled. "I guess I will name him later."

I was about to expound on the wonderful qualities of the name Alan when I heard the bedroom door open. The much-too-late paramedics had arrived. "Good work, Al!" they shouted, slapping my back. "We'll take her to the hospital to deliver the placenta."

"The what?" I asked, not quite remembering that part of my police academy movie.

"It's what is attached to the other end of the cord. Why don't you get cleaned up and meet us at the hospital?"

I did go to the hospital. I even had a few pictures taken with the baby and Anne. As I was walked out the door, back to my patrol unit, I said to myself, I will call him Alan, anyway.

THE GANDY DANCER

MARTIN DONAHUE STOOD UNDER THE MERCURY STREET LIGHT with his arms folded tightly across his chest in a showdown posture. As I approached in the patrol car, I could see his stern expression and his bright white hair glowing above his wrinkled face. He looked like an angry old man wearing a Halloween mask. His jaw was set at confrontation level and his eyes said that he was already angry about how I would handle his complaint. I took a little longer than necessary to check out with my dispatcher and to make a note in my daily log. I wanted to prolong, as much as I could, dealing with my least-favorite complainant.

He glared at me with contempt and began to pace under the light. Although I wanted to try, there would be no avoiding Martin Donahue tonight.

"Hello Mr. Donahue," I said, closing my car door and walking to him under the light. "What seems to be the problem?"

"You deaf or something? Can't you hear them?" Martin said in his best angry and annoyed voice. He looked north and sighed. "Been going on ever since dark. Like to think our crack police force would notice such flagrant violations."

With Martin's pause I could faintly hear the occasional pop of firecrackers and the hiss of bottle rockets being launched in the darkness. Most were several blocks away, but some seemed nearly around the corner. I concentrated intently on the sounds, enjoying the few moments of relief from Martin's antagonistic voice. "I hear them, Martin," I said slowly. "The problem is that being the Fourth of July, it's hard to control everyone with the holiday spirit. Their stocks will run low by tomorrow night."

"The *problem*, Officer White, is that you are ignoring obvious violations of state law. I didn't know that the fireworks statutes were suspended during our nation's birthday."

"Not suspended Martin, just tolerated a little. Look, some of the people who went to Florida last winter stopped off in other states where they are legal and bought them at roadside stands. The fireworks have been sitting in their garage or basement or wherever until tonight, and now their kids are having a little fun. When it gets a little blatant we confiscate their stash and give a warning. Occasionally we will issue some citations to holders of the more advanced pyrotechnics."

"You, sir, have a duty to enforce *all* laws, regardless of your personal feelings. I demand that you arrest these people!" He put his hands on his hips and stared at me, hoping for a challenge.

"I'll tell you what, Mr. Donahue. I'll spend some time in the neighborhood and quiet things down. If I see any blatant violations, I'll take action."

"I don't like your attitude, young man. Rest assured, I will call your chief."

I said nothing and returned to my patrol car. To argue my point would only further anger Martin and this, of course, is what he enjoyed.

Martin Donahue's world was divided equally between what he despised and what he wanted to despise, but had yet to find a good reason. He was somewhere between the ages of eighty-five and angel of death. At times I thought his anger and contempt for the human race were the only things keeping him from the far end of the scale.

Martin loved to be unhappy. This fact was obvious to anyone with whom he came in contact. Most of his time seemed to be spent looking for things to complain about, or become angry at. Because of this, he was quite well known in the community. He reported any violation, no matter how trivial, and demanded immediate police action. Any officer not satisfying his demands was reported to the chief or city manager. Receiving a Donahue call, as they were known, was a reason to cringe. There was no pleasing this man.

Aside from his neighborhood watchdog approach to borderline violations, Martin also showed his community support, or lack of community support, in other areas. He attended each city commission meeting and railed against everything from taxes to planned developments. It seemed that no one besides Martin Donahue knew how things should be run. When not aggravating or verbally accosting public servants and elected officials, Martin used his time to write letters to the editors of local papers. These written comments were so common that the majority of the citizens ignored any legitimate point he might have made. In my police community, it was considered a kind of honor to be mentioned in a Donahue letter.

What free time this public complaining left for Martin, was spent in his garage. Nearly every night on patrol, I would spot the yellow glow of work lights coming from his large, single-car garage. He was normally slumped over a table working on something or standing next to a large power saw. It was hard to imagine Martin with a woodworking hobby, but at least he took a break from his civic disturbances.

After the release of *Alaska Behind Blue Eyes*, I became aware of the community interest in a working police officer who is also an author. I was not prepared for all the attention. To me, I was just . . . me. I put words on paper and luckily people seemed to like my literary rambling.

By the start of the following school year I began to receive requests from school districts all over Michigan to speak to their students. Most of the time I talked to young author groups, giving the budding authors encouragement to pursue their writing dreams. It seemed strange to be elevated on the pedestal of published writer. My chief was very patient and supportive when I asked for time off to travel to many remote schools.

One day I traveled to the west side of the state, to a tiny district tucked between the sand hills and the shore of Lake Michigan. It was a small school with kindergarten through twelfth grade in one building. I spent the morning talking about rejection slips from publishing companies and what it is like to see my book in print. As always, the kids were full of questions. By lunchtime I still had two classes to go before completing my tour. After eating lunch with the principal in the crowded cafeteria, she treated me to a tour of the school.

Near the end of the hallway came the infectious sound of children laughing. Their giggles were mixed with the tapping sound of wood against wood. I was immediately intrigued and took several steps before turning back toward the principal.

"It's Gandy Dancer," she said with a big smile. "He comes here every year to entertain the younger students. We're lucky to have him come to a school this small. I know he is in great demand. Go take a look."

I looked in through the open door to see a man standing before a long table. He was wearing an old-fashioned cobbler costume, complete with a feathered cap. He held the crossed wooden bars in each hand and skillfully moved the marionettes across the table as if they were alive. He followed their actions with his giddy voice, telling the story and completely captivating his young audience. At times he would nearly dance along with the dolls, becoming part of the show. I looked at the children's faces as they followed the action. Wild eyes beamed toward their entertainer with glee. Never had I watched someone so completely captivate such young children. I was jealous of his ability. As he turned to pick up another marionette I saw his face.

Looking back at me, under the floppy hat with the feather in the band, was the face of Martin Donahue.

I backed away from the room like someone who had just seen a large grizzly bear and was trying to retreat without being noticed. "That's Martin Donahue!" I said to the principal.

"Isn't he wonderful?" she answered, looking through the door. "The children love him. He's from your hometown, you know."

"I . . . know," I said, still not believing that Martin was smiling, let alone making children happy.

"He makes the marionettes himself, along with all the other props. Martin's been coming here for many years now. I forget exactly how many. I just love the sense of joy he brings to the children."

This was too weird. I almost caught myself liking Martin Donahue for a moment. The dark foreboding image I kept in my mind was slowly beginning to soften, like water dissolving a sand sculpture. In defense, I tried to fight back. "Well . . . do you know anything about his personal life?" I asked the principal, in a tone she found confusing. Her face showed some concern, then turned sorrowful.

"Oh, you mean about the accident."

"The accident?"

"It hurt him deeply. For years he felt no reason to live. Martin calls it his dark time. If it were not for his love of children he may have killed himself."

"What happened?" I asked, my anger at Martin slowly turning to curiosity.

"It was years ago, long before you were born. A drunk driver killed his wife and young son. Some small-town politician with a lot of connections was coming from some party and ran a red light. It happened when they lived in Indiana. The guy got off with almost nothing for punishment. It seemed that the whole community wanted to protect this guy. Years later, Martin's job took him to Michigan."

"That's terrible. But why doesn't he perform for the kids in Clare?"

"I assumed that he did," she answered.

"No. He never does."

"Strange. Maybe he doesn't want people to know that he can be happy. Anger is very hard to let go. It could be that he feels his hometown people would not understand."

I wanted to march into the classroom and let Martin see me. I wanted him to know that I knew about his past and that, as much as he would hate it, acknowledge that he had a wonderful soft side. But I didn't. I was still thinking about the Gandy Dancer when I walked across the parking lot to my truck, dreading the long ride home.

"Officer White," came a voice from behind. It was the unmistakable voice of Martin Donahue. "Did you enjoy the show?" he asked in his usual gruff voice, leaving the upbeat tones of Gandy Dancer in the school.

"You have a gift, Mr. Donahue, perhaps more than you know. Come to our school. Let the kids experience your talent. It's a disservice to the community to keep it from them." I was being far too bold, but with my current knowledge of Martin I had the advantage.

"*You don't think that I want to visit our school?* I could be down there every day. It's just . . ."

"What?"

"Maybe I enjoy being a pain in the ass."

"No! That's not it. Tell me the truth or I'll take pictures of your next performance and have them published in our local paper."

"Officer White, I have, at one time or another, angered everyone in town. It is their children that would see Gandy Dancer. How would that *look*?"

"It would *look* like there is more to Martin Donahue than an angry old man."

"You don't *understand*."

"I'll tell you what I *understand*, Mr. Donahue. I understand that before today I didn't like you. Now you just disappoint me." I turned around quickly and got into my truck. Martin was walking away as I left for home. The Martin Donahue that I thought I knew walked off to his car, while the Gandy Dancer's spirit remained in the hearts of the children.

LAUNDROMAT SURVIVALIST

BEFORE I LEFT MY MICHIGAN HOMELAND FOR ALASKA, SOMEONE else washed my clothes. My mother took responsibility for the majority of my formative years, until a fairly anal-retentive roommate came along who liked schedules and order, and enjoyed my helplessness when it came to domestic matters such as laundry. Bud, my roommate, kept up with the household chores fairly well, until we both acquired girlfriends who, among other things, enjoyed having us wear clothes that were unwrinkled and smelled nice. In a way, it was a perfect arrangement. The girls would come to our apartment, be repulsed at the way we lived, make a few comments about the helplessness of men in general, and then hose out the place.

My first apartment in Skagway, Alaska was the size of a fishing shanty and, by coincidence, had a similar odor. On the rare occasions when I actually vacuumed, which was only before having company and even then only of the special kind, I could do the entire apartment from the same electrical outlet, and basically from the same spot in the center of the room. The problem with living quarters this small was that it left little space to hide things, such as the growing pile of dirty clothes taking up precious space in the center of the room. I decided to use the camouflage method of hiding the pile by tucking a plain-colored blanket over it and making it look like a lumpy beanbag chair. As the pile grew to the proportions of a major league pitching mound and emitted the fragrance of a wet dog, the rest of my wearable clothes were assessed into various stages of *clean*.

One thing that all single men share is the ability to pick clothes by using the air-it-and- wear-it method. I would smell each item before putting it on to judge if it could be worn based on what I was going to do that day. Eventually, however, even carefully hanging my clothes on doorknobs and out the window was not enough to keep up with my dismal social schedule. I would have to visit the Laundromat.

Skagway had one Laundromat that was used by nearly everyone who did not have the money or the desire to acquire a washer and dryer. It was located on the city's main street and served as a bastion of cleanliness for the great unwashed of this tiny northern community. Because of my before-mentioned aversion to doing laundry, I would enter the building with nearly all of my clothes stuffed in trash bags, looking like Santa Claus, except I was lugging in smelly clothing instead of gifts.

To be honest, I liked the way the Laundromat smelled. The building was warm inside and had the heavy moist odor of fabric softener. The constant hum and soft drone of the machines was lulling and it smelled like home. Long, yellow tables were set up near the row of churning appliances, allowing me an opportunity to, well, air my dirty laundry. This was always a rather embarrassing thing for me. It was one thing to keep my soiled items hidden in the safety of my tiny apartment, but quite another to display them to the community at large. At times I felt as if I should wash my clothes in my bathtub first, to have them in some acceptable stage of *clean* before taking them out in public. I didn't, however. That would have been too much like washing the dishes before putting them in the dishwasher.

It was especially embarrassing for me because I was known to the community as a police officer. The public's fascination with law enforcement extended to a curiosity of what I wore off duty and under my uniform. Whenever a local kid walked by my table and made a flip comment about my boxer shorts embroidered with various dry flies I'd cringe.

Bud, who had moved to Wichita, Kansas, said that Laundromats were a great place to meet women. He suggested that I put all of my clothes in one giant lump on a table and make a statement indicating that I would wash them all together. His theory was that a young, single, and helpful woman would jump to the rescue and sort them for me, thus starting a conversation and, hopefully, a long or even brief relationship. I found several flaws in this idea, however. The first was that this *was* how I washed my clothes. The second was that women in the "mat" didn't seem to care, except for a couple of elderly sisters who viewed the Laundromat experience as an opportunity to gossip. (I did learn a lot about the darker side of Skagway from them.)

I found the collection of people brought together in a Laundromat was also very interesting. For someone with a mind like mine, this was a rich wood lot of slightly bent trees. The tables in the corner were usually where the throwbacks to the hippy generation sorted through their clothes and their equally wrinkled social agendas. The tables nearest the door attracted single dock workers and ship crewmen, so they could quickly run to the bar next door for a quick one between loads. On the far side, the seasonal workers in town sorted through a long summer's worth of business clothes. And, in the center, a collection of talkative old women and misfits like me watched it all happen.

I began making Saturday night my time for visiting the mat. This was partly because of my work schedule, but mostly because of my lack of any social agenda. With nothing better to do, I viewed each trip as an event. I made plans to read, write, and listen to music on my new portable CD player. At first I didn't talk much, instead I chose to listen to the rapid-fire and unusual conversation that dirty garments and long Alaskan nights could bring. Before long, however, I joined in with the group. After the initial embarrassment wore off, I confidently strutted into the building and took my favorite table in the back. I became a Laundromat survivalist.

One Saturday night I was dealing with a rather large pile of dirty items left over from a two-week absence. I had learned to separate my clothes into piles by their color and odor. I laid them along the yellow table. It was a busy night in the mat, being the tourist season. (In the summer the population of Skagway more than doubles with people who come to Alaska to work the tourist trade.) While my first batch of soiled threads churned in the machine I began working on my uniform shirts. Because of my ability to sweat profusely, even in the cool climate of an Alaskan summer, the collars of my work shirts needed special attention. Using a trick I learned from a mat veteran, I put spot remover along each collar and began scrubbing them with a small soft brush. When I was on shirt number three, *she* walked in the door.

She was the very embodiment of beauty. Just looking at her as she walked through the crowded room sent tingles down my spine. She was nearly six feet tall with long sandy hair that hung just over her shoulders. Her face was like something out of a beauty magazine, and held a soft allure that was irresistible for a lonely officer far from home. *She* had that I'm-comfortable-anywhere look as she strolled forward. Her blue eyes hit mine like a fist. An oh-so-soft white tee shirt was tucked into her tan shorts, leaving about four feet of tanned legs between them and her hiking boots. I tried to act nonchalant, something that was difficult when faced with such a creature. I continued scrubbing the collar without looking away from her face, trying to make eye contact. She walked toward me with a confident step, looking for an open spot on a table. Currently my table was full with mounds of my soiled clothes and also occupied by Mrs. Hanson, who was in the process of explaining the virtues of spot removers.

Then it happened. The object of my desire, indeed my every fantasy, looked at me with a huge smile that bordered on mirth. I could feel her eyes upon me as I tried to look relaxed, which was difficult at best, while frantically scrubbing my uniform shirt collar and sending her my best single-and- available power-glance. Captivated by her obvious interest in me, I wondered if it was my almost rippling muscles as I moved the brush rapidly. Or, perhaps, it was my dignified look of an officer and a gentleman. Slowly she walked toward me with a giant smile and piercing blue eyes. When she was in striking distance from my table, I cleared my throat to say hello, only to be stopped by her burst of laughter. I will never forget the way she let out with a belly laugh that filled the Laundromat with joy. She slowed to a giggle and pointed at my crotch.

"Must be a tough stain," she said with the deadpan delivery of a professional comedian. She then walked away and took an open spot at a table behind me.

Mrs. Hanson looked down also and began to laugh like a little girl. I lowered my head and found that my aggressive scrubbing had resulted in a large pile of white foam that hung on my crotch like a fluffy softball. When Mrs. Hanson regained her composure, she looked at me with forced seriousness. "My, Officer White, that young lady certainly had quite an affect on you." She gleefully broke into a giggle fit, along with most of the mat patrons.

As quickly as I could, I finished my laundry and prepared to leave. Feeling the stares of about thirty smiling people as I headed for the door, I turned around for one final word.

"I meant to do that!" I shouted over the churning machines.

SHALL WE GATHER

M Y FRIEND BUD LEANED WITH ME AGAINST THE PATROL CAR and looked at the hickory tree. Although over three feet in diameter, the huge tree was snapped off about twenty feet from the ground, like a giant boot had given it a grand kick. One of the larger limbs went through the roof of a house all the way to the floor. Behind the hickory, a three-hundred-foot path of broken-off and overturned trees lay as far as we could see. I folded my arms across my chest and looked at my friend. "Tornado?" I asked.

"Nope."

"You sure?"

"Yes."

"How?"

"See how all the trees are laying in the same direction? They're all pointed east. That west wind from the storm pushed them over. I used to live in Kansas, remember? Tornado alley." Bud pointed beyond the hickory tree to a group of large spruce scattered on the ground. "I saw a lot of tornado damage around Wichita. Tornadoes spread debris and trees and buildings, and even farm animals, in all directions. They sometimes cut narrow paths, but without any order. Besides, were any mobile homes destroyed?"

"None that I know of."

"See, more proof. Tornadoes always go for the trailers." Bud laughed and kicked at a fallen branch.

"Buy why not everywhere? Why only this narrow path?"

"It's called straight-line wind damage. It has to do with the differences in pressure and temperature in the storm's air masses. The combination creates a giant burst of wind energy that slams the earth with hurricane force winds that level everything in its path. Luckily for Clare, no one was killed."

I got into my patrol unit and settled behind the wheel. Bud walked to my open window and leaned against the car, looking forward to the overturned trees. "I better go," I said, putting the car in drive. "There's not a lot I can do except drive around and look important. People like to see the patrol car out, especially on a day like today." Bud waved goodbye and walked to his vehicle. *Straight-line wind*, I thought, as I drove down the street.

It was the kind of storm that always seems to strike other communities, the type that moves across the state reeking havoc in other small towns while Clare receives only heavy rain. But not this time. The evening before began calm, with warm sticky air and still skies. By nightfall the sky had turned a pale yellow and the humidity increased like a warning of doom. The weather report called for scattered storms, some of which could be intense. By the time darkness fell, most people assumed the risk was over. We were all wrong.

After midnight the wind picked up, and then came the thunder. Lightning flashed like anger over our small town. I stood by my bedroom window watching the rain come down sideways, turning the country road into a river. It was over in an hour.

In the gray of morning, I surveyed the damage around my house. I was lucky. There were a few broken limbs laying around and some trash blown in from elsewhere, but nothing serious, except for the lack of power. The electricity was out in my entire neighborhood, but I assumed this would be corrected soon. Little did I know that living three miles from Clare, had spared my home.

In town the damage was significant. I drove to work that morning and saw a scene normally reserved for news broadcasts. The winds from the night before had ripped through Clare, toppling great trees and tearing shingles from roofs. Power lines had been ripped from their poles and lay across streets covered in tree limbs. Electricity was out in the entire city plus for miles in all directions.

I had never been without electricity for more than a few hours in my life. It is in times like this that one fully understands how dependent we are on electrical power. Living in the country, losing power to my house meant more than a lack of lights and electrical appliances. It meant no water. I came home from work that day to find Ken, my neighbor, struggling with a large assortment of plastic containers. Most were empty milk jugs and a few were insulated coolers.

"Hi neighbor!" Ken shouted from across the street. He put the jugs into a large trash bag and walked toward me. "I think there's enough for both of us." Ken crossed the road and tossed the sack into the back of my truck.

"Find someone out here that still has power?" I asked.

"Nah, we'll go to the flowing well out on Beaverton Road," Ken said. "Better water than home anyway."

"I'll go inside and change. Just give me a few minutes," I said, dreading the upcoming days of toting water.

The flowing well, as Ken and everyone else called it, was nothing more than an old pipe sticking out of the ground with a ninety-degree joint pointed toward the road. Ground water under pressure flowed through the pipe, creating a small stream that eventually joined the Tobacco River system. When I was a kid, my friends and I used to ride our bikes in this area and would always stop at the well for a cool drink. I also remembered that this water always tasted better than the water at home. With the power out in most of Clare County, this well would provide locals with an uninterrupted source of fresh water.

Ken and I drove along the country roads toward the well. We passed many houses and farms. Everywhere people were using the sunny evening to clean up downed branches, and in many cases, entire trees. The empty jugs in the back of my truck bounced and rattled as we went over the gravel roads.

"Kind of like stepping back in time," Ken said. He looked out the window distantly, leaving his words like a question.

"What do you mean?"

"A hundred years ago everyone used outside wells. Most would have hand pumps on their property, naturally flowing wells near their homes would have been a luxury. Now we only use them in times of crisis. They're kind of unappreciated."

As I drove down Beaverton Road and came in sight of the well, I thought back to Ken's previous statement. "Looks like this one's now over-appreciated," I said quietly.

"Wow," Ken answered, leaning forward in the truck seat.

What used to be a quiet section of road was now a parking lot. Cars, trucks, and sport utility vehicles lined the road on each side for two hundred feet. Judging by the vehicles, a complete cross-section of our small community was assembled at the well. Battered old pickup trucks were parked in front of shiny new cars, with sporty vehicles owned by younger drivers sitting alongside conservative dark suburbans. Bumper and window stickers ranged from "Fear This," to "My Child is an Honor Roll Student." Ken was impressed.

"What modern conveniences pull apart, water brings together," he said.

I parked behind a truck with a bed full of freshly cut tree limbs. Ken and I took the bags of empty jugs and began walking along the line of vehicles toward the well. Off to our right, several young children were playing a game of tag while some older kids were tossing a football. From the back of a sport utility vehicle, a middle-aged woman was showing off photos of her grandchildren to several older ladies. As we passed, more photos were brought out, creating an impromptu gallery. Behind them other children were picking wildflowers that were growing in the ditch.

Nearing the well, we could see a crowd of men and women talking. Hands were being shaken and backs were being slapped. The mood was more like an ice cream social than a quest for water. We reached the crowd surrounding the well and stopped behind a group of men who were playfully arguing over which brand of truck was best for farm work. Beyond them one of my old schoolteachers was filling his containers, holding his tie out of the way while discussing the current state of education with a teen wearing camouflage pants. The young man was listened intently, while helping my teacher ready the next containers to be filled. Next in line was a farmer who was in the process of telling a well-dressed businessman just how the Detroit Lions could, if they took his advice, make it to the Super Bowl. A rather plump woman worked through the group with a batch of warm cookies just as my old teacher filled his last jug. Two young men ran forward and helped him carry the containers to his car. The farmer was still talking about the problems with the NFL as he began filling his containers. Ken set his bag on the ground and pulled me aside.

"You know," Ken said, looking around at the milling people, "this is really nice. Without the loss of power, all these people would be at home, or at work. I wonder when was the last time that all these people got together and talked with their neighbors."

I looked at the crowd, then back to Ken. "Notice what is not here?"

"Our local weatherman apologizing?" Ken asked, laughing.

"What's not here are the negative emotions. Look around. There's no aggravation, annoyance, anger, or disappointment. Nothing like that. These aren't people reacting to a tragedy. This is a township picnic."

It was nearly three hours later before Ken and I had our jugs filled and were heading back to our homes. We left the well with a few more handshakes and promises to keep in touch—and a feeling that we wanted to come back.

Three days later the power company crews had restored power to most of the county. Once again our lives were back to a comfortable routine. I was glad for the convenience, but inside I secretly wished that I could return to the well, back to a simpler time when neighbors gathered and relied on each other because of a longing to share their lives and not because of a bad event.

Weeks later I drove by the well. There were no vehicles parked along the road and the water flowed uninterrupted from the old pipe. I felt a sense of loss because we were back to dealing with life as individuals. The old well brought back, at least for a time, the comfortable feeling that we all need each other.

Considering Nola

"**Y**OU CAN SEE IT FROM THIS WINDOW, OFFICER." NOLA pushed hard against the chrome runner of the wheelchair and moved ahead several feet. She pushed again, leaning forward in the chair, as if to use the momentum of her frail body to speed across the tan carpet. At the window she reached forward and pulled the white drapes back. "Can you see what they did?" she asked. Nola released the drapes, but kept her long index finger pointing toward the glass. Her skin was stretched tightly over her body; it was nearly transparent. I could see each vein and blemish, like the teaching models we used in high school anatomy class. She lowered her arm and folded it with the other across her chest.

I looked out the window at the tiny garden plot provided by the adult foster care home. A five by five-foot square section in front of her window broke the green of the manicured lawn. Where the ground used to be thick with marigolds, now only a few dying greens remained amid the bicycle tracks. The earth was dark and rich in the small garden. I could tell it was well cared for by the lack of weeds and the sharp edges cut into the lawn.

"They did it intentionally, Officer White," Nola said quietly. "It was the boys from the complex across the street. They make fun of me in the parking lot sometimes. And, before you ask, no, I did not see them do it. But I know."

I backed across the faded tan carpet and sat on a vinyl ottoman across the room. Nola had decorated her one-bedroom apartment with cheap Jesus prints in large, gold plastic frames. A small, round table stood in the center of the room. It was covered with junk mail and grocery coupons. From my seat I could still see the battered remains of the garden through the window. Taking out my small writing pad, I began to take notes for my report.

"Why do they torment me, Officer White?" Nola asked, rolling away from the window and moving in front of me. She moved her tiny hands to her head and pulled off her glasses, bringing them to rest in her lap. "Nathan, the maintenance man, tilled that spot just for me. He said that the owner would not approve, but he did it anyway."

I finished my notes and looked back out the window. "They are still selling flats of flowers downtown. This time of year they are even discounted," I said, trying to help.

"I ordered the seeds from a catalog last winter. I grew them in Styrofoam cups until Mother's Day. Jan, from next door, planted the seedlings for me. She even took me outside and let me plant a few myself. I can see no point in purchasing store-bought flowers now."

"Do you know the names of the boys?" I asked.

"No. They play basketball over in the playground almost every night. One boy is heavy and always wears black shorts. The other is much smaller. They ride small fancy bikes. You can find them if you try," Nola said distantly. "That is, if you want to."

Nola McGovern was born with a disease that no one could pronounce. *She* could, of course, and would at any opportunity if questioned about the nature of her illness. It was a rare condition that had left her with a small stunted body since childhood. Her parents died when she was quite young, and Nola had spent the last thirty years in different institutions. Several years ago, at the age of fifty-five, she was moved to this assisted living home.

Nola's disease attacked her body at the speed of a glacier, making each year just a little more physically challenging than the one before. Now her muscles were almost destroyed and even getting around in a wheelchair was difficult. The wonder, or the cruelty, depending on how you looked at it, was that her mind still functioned normally. This left her with a very sharp mind, trapped within a useless shell of weakness and pain.

Nola was not a happy person, not that anyone in her debilitated condition would be, and she shared this fact with everyone she met. To her visiting healthcare providers she was stubborn and antagonistic. From her wheelchair she would direct each visit as a necessary inconvenience, to the point that many refused to return. Social agencies were constantly recruiting replacements for the frustrated workers. Nola seemed not to care, realizing that, like it or not, they were obligated to address her needs. So, she took advantage of these kind people, almost as though her actions were somehow justified by her pain.

"The kids have no idea how lucky they are," Nola said sternly. She turned her wheelchair to face me and looked down at her nearly useless body. "They can run and jump and play without fear of falling or senseless teasing. Their bodies do as they wish. It is such a shame that they take this for granted."

"I know how you must feel," I empathized, looking out the window at the ruined flower bed.

"*You* know how I feel?" she shouted. Nola leaned back and let her head rest against the vinyl chair back. A mixture of mirth and anger came over her face. I realized I had insulted her. "How could you possibly *know*, Officer White?"

"I mean . . ."

"What you *mean*, Officer White, is that you want to leave. You have now taken the required report, quite professionally I must admit, and now you are trying to say some sympathetic words to soothe the old cripple before you depart. You, Officer White, cannot imagine being like me, and you know it. In a few minutes you will be in your air-conditioned car driving around and waiting for your next call. After work you will go home and do anything you wish. You have no physical limitations to restrict your actions. You can run if you please, or walk, or swim, but you will think nothing of your ability to do these things. And, you will not think of me, other than the fact that I can be a pain in the ass."

I tried to speak, but no words would come. Nola rolled back to the window and stared blankly outside. "I would like to run. I know that must seem funny to you, but ever since childhood I wanted to run. There was a tree behind our farm. It was a giant oak that grew skyward from the pasture. I could see it from my bedroom window and I fantasized about running across the field and climbing to the highest branches. It was always my dream, on most nights anyway, except for boys. Yes, Officer White, I did think about boys. I tried to talk about being married with my mother, but she would give me a patronizing speech, as if I had suggested space travel. I've never had a boyfriend, or a date, for that matter. You must think this odd, that an old cripple would want to feel a man in her bed. By now you must be embarrassed, or at least think that I would be embarrassed admitting this fact, but I am not. At least I have the courage to admit the truth."

I folded my notepad and ceremoniously put it in my pocket. "I will try to find the boys, Nola. I will let you know what happens."

"Yes," Nola said quietly. "Let me know what happens."

I did drive around in my patrol car, enjoying the air conditioning and my freedom of movement. That night at home, I took a walk down my road and tried to understand what Nola felt. Although I thought of many ways that my body could be improved, the limitless freedom I had was heartening. Try as I might, I could not imagine being restricted to a wheelchair.

About a quarter-mile down the road from my house is a green pasture complete with a large oak tree. I looked at it differently that night as I thought of Nola. Soon I was walking across the green alfalfa, feeling the thickness of the crop rubbing against my shoes. The thick, sweet smell drifted up from the ground softly, as I walked slowly toward the tree. *Nola would like this tree,* I thought. The large trunk was blackened with age and its thick, heavy branches spread out like a green canopy. I sat at its base and leaned back against the trunk, thinking of some way to make Nola happy, at least for once in her life.

The hallway was quiet as I made my way to Nola's door. My unannounced visit was not without a great deal of planning, most of which involved speaking with the owner of the pasture. I shifted the multicolored bouquet of carnations from my right to left hand and confidently knocked on the door, putting on my best smile. Moments later I heard the familiar sound of her wheelchair coming across the carpet and stopping at the door. She turned the deadbolt and pulled the door open.

"Officer White," Nola said in an annoyed tone. "I expected you might return. Being that you are not in uniform and holding a rather nice collection of flowers, I can assume that this is not a professional visit." She wheeled backwards to allow me in, stopping at her kitchen table. I had expected a smile, but she only gave me her standard depressed expression.

"Nola, I am here to ask you out for a date. There is a beautiful pasture near my house, with a large oak tree. I packed a picnic lunch and thought I could take you there. You will love the place." I waited for her response and continued with my broad smile.

"Well, well, Officer White. You certainly know how to handle people, *don't you*? All your police training has served you well. A gentleman officer sees, what he believes to be, a problem and develops a plan of action." Nola brought her hands together, forming a steeple with her fingers. She stared at her fingertips and pressed them tightly against each other.

"I thought we could spend the afternoon together. I would like to get you out of here for a while and have the chance to know you better."

"And, since you assumed that I would have nothing better to do, you decided to give me some relief from my otherwise dismal life. Of course, you expect me to jump at the opportunity for a little farm frolic."

"It will be fun. We can . . ."

"Officer White," Nola said, looking up from her hands and into my eyes. "Do you really believe that I can be pleased by your proposal? You come to my home, unannounced, with your sympathetic confidence and patronizing sincerity without truly understanding the real reason for this visit. The *real reason* you appear at my door is to ease your nagging guilt. You cannot imagine what an insult this is to me! Your wife and officer friends must think of you as a hero for doing something kind for the old cripple. At least twenty people must be aware of your scheme, which hinges on my acceptance of your offer. Well, Officer White, I shall not go with you. You may be a fine and professional officer, but I have no use or time for guilt-forced charity. Your fantasies of giving me one day of open air and pleasure were flawed because you considered everyone's feelings but mine. Just find and punish the children responsible for damaging my flowers. That is all I want from you. Now, please go away."

The smile had long-since drained from my face. Inside I felt terrible, but I also had a yearning to argue my point. It was then that I realized that no matter how honorable my intentions were, they did not make up for the lack of consideration for Nola's feelings. I quickly turned and started for the door.

"Officer White," Nola said sternly. "You may leave the flowers."

WINGED CONFUSION

AUGUST IS A DIFFICULT AND CHALLENGING TIME FOR MICHIGAN'S little brown bats. I know this from extensive research, which mainly consisted of asking people why the scary brown things always seemed to be most active in homes this time of year. You see, August is when juvenile bats leave the safety of their hiding spots for the first time to venture into the world of insect sucking. Like all teen critters, the young bats often become misguided and take the wrong route. People who otherwise are unaware that their homes are used as breeding grounds for sailing rodents suddenly find themselves face-to-face with misdirected young bats. Like all other youths of small communities, the bats want desperately to get out.

As a veteran bat evictor and youthful mammal supervisor, I consider the "bat calls" just another unusual part of my role as a police officer. Although I pride myself on a long list of successful evictions, I never quite understood why people call the police when a flapping invader flies through their kitchen. I assume that when faced with any scary problem, people call the police to solve what they lack the knowledge to do on their own. Or, as is probably the case, what they do not want to do on their own. In any event, call me Alan, the bat expert.

One particular encounter happened on a sticky late-August night. My dispatcher gave the address slowly, as if doing so would ease my apprehension about the call. It was in the older part of town, where most of the houses were built for large families, which were common at that time. I pulled into the driveway and recognized the house as being owned by an elderly widow who liked to work in her flowerbeds. We had never formally met, but had a good wave-as-you-drive-by relationship. The old woman always seemed to be outside. She was a wonderful gardener.

Another thing that I remembered was her appearance. No matter how actively she worked the ground or raked the leaves or even shoveled the walk, she was always dressed neatly. She had an air of dignity at all times, even when taking out the garbage. "Good afternoon, Officer," she would say to the slowly passing patrol car while looking up from weeding her plants. I looked forward to helping her with her bat problem.

The porch light shined brightly in the dark as I made my way up the perfectly edged walk. I entered the porch, admiring the many hanging plants and polished figurines neatly placed on several small tables. After three sharp knocks, I could hear her quickly walking across the floor to the large wooden front door. With a brief squeak the door opened quickly, flooding the porch with bright light from the living room.

The first thing I noticed was how small she was. Since I had only seen her from the front seat of my patrol car, I had not realized her true size. At six feet I towered over her by at least a foot. Her face was streaked with perspiration that ran down in tiny streams to the collar of her bright pink bathrobe. Normally her hair was neatly styled, but now it fell from her head with many wet strands pasted over her forehead. She was breathing rapidly, as if she had run a mile or two or three. She licked her lips and tried to catch her breath to speak. In her right hand she held at quarter arms a bright yellow fly swatter that was decorated with a red ladybug. "Good evening, ma'am," I said slowly, trying not to laugh. She turned away from me without speaking, using the fly swatter as a pointer.

"It's in there," she gasped, directing me to the dining room with the swatter. She stepped back to allow me to enter. She paused. "I did my best," she said.

I walked through the living room, admiring the polished surface of the antique tables and the stateliness of the ten-foot ceiling. A large brass chandelier hung on a golden chain over a coffee table of rich mahogany. My book, *Alaska Behind Blue Eyes*, rested on the table with several magazines. I wanted to turn and ask if she had enjoyed my first book, but something in the way she stood, hiding in the corner, told me to save the question for another time.

The dining room was elegant. Thick beige carpet flowed across the large room under a giant oak table and matching chairs. A white tablecloth with intricate designs adorned the table, along with a brass vase filled with fresh flowers.

"Do you see it?" she asked, peaking around the door.

"Not yet," I answered, stepping further into the room. The walls were covered in a dignified white and silver wallpaper that led to a white textured ceiling. I scanned the corners of the room looking for the bat. Because Michigan's little brown bats, when not in flight, are about the size of a folded playing card, they are sometimes difficult to spot. Seeing nothing, I turned around to check on my complainant and saw a small patch of brown over the door casing.

I walked closer and watched as the little bat clung to the wall, blending in with the dark wood trim. I studied the shiny brown fur over its body and the black wings tightly folded at its sides. I almost laughed out loud because the little animal was breathing nearly as hard as the woman. I wasn't sure who was more in need of rest. "It's right over this door," I whispered. The woman stepped back from the doorway like a child from a beehive.

"What are you going to do?" she asked, still moving back with the fly swatter in front of her perspiring face.

"Don't worry, ma'am," I confidently said. "The little guy will be gone in a moment. I will have to close this door, though. I don't want him to get into the rest of the house."

"I agree," she said from across the living room where she was hiding behind the couch.

I closed the door between the living room and the dining room. Now, just the bat and me shared the elegant space. I walked to the opposite side of the room and opened the large door to the kitchen. As I had hoped, the kitchen had many windows. I shut the door behind me and began to take plants down from the sills and to remove the curtains. Then I opened all the windows and removed the screens. Satisfied there was ample room for escape, I returned to the dining room.

The bat was still recovering above the casing as I approached. "Ma'am," I said, hoping she could hear me. A muffled voice came from the living room.

"Yes, officer," she said slowly.

"You are going to hear some loud noises, but don't worry. Okay?"

"Okay," was her response.

I jumped up as high as I could and slapped the wall hard with a loud BANG. As expected, the little bat lifted from the wall and began fluttering around the room. I was amazed, as always, how bats can negotiate objects in such tight quarters. It flew around the chandelier several times, dipping and climbing in large circles. I walked to the center of the room and began clapping my hands and yelling loudly, trying to push the animal toward the open kitchen door. Frightened by the noise, the bat left the room and began flying about the kitchen. I ran forward, closing the door behind me.

From the back of the kitchen I again clapped and yelled, occasionally ducking as the bat made strafing runs over my head. About a minute later it found an open window and sailed into the darkness. I quickly closed the windows, then went to check on the woman.

I found her still hiding behind the couch with an afghan draped over her body. I tried to restrain a smile. "You can come out now," I said.

Together we put the plants back on the windowsills and replaced the curtains. The woman put the last plant in place and looked at me.

"I don't like bats," she said.

HEXAGENIA'S
AND JIMMY HENDRIX

T HE BRIEF RAIN HAD STOPPED AN HOUR AGO AND WAS REPLACED
by clear skies and a sun that would turn the June afternoon
into the kind of heat that would be unbearable, if I was not
about to do something I loved. The humidity and the heat made me
feel like I was standing in a giant terrarium. To compound my dis-
comfort I was wearing chest waders and a heavy fishing vest. Sweat
ran down my face in a constant stream, while my glasses fogged in
the thick, heavy air. In the west the sun glowed copper-yellow as it
slowly descended, hesitantly, as if not wanting to give up on the heat.
Larry pointed to a well-worn path with the tip of his fly rod as he
brushed sweat from his forehead with his other hand.

"We cut through the woods here. It's about a mile to the best
holes."

I nodded, but said nothing, saving my strength for the upcoming
humid hike. We walked down the trail and into a deep forest of pines
and cedars. It seemed a little cooler under the trees, but I still wished
that I had packed my gear in rather than donning my waders on this
blistering day.

The trail snaked among the trees and crossed several small creeks before straightening and crossing a meadow. Thick grasses grew tall in the rich soil, casting a heavy smell that hung like nature's perfume in the late afternoon. White and yellow wildflowers bloomed along the trail, while bees collected nectar from their blossoms before the fall of night.

We entered another patch of woods on the far side of the meadow and followed an old two-track logging trail. After another quarter-mile Larry stopped and pointed toward a faint path that led to the left.

"I'll walk in from here. Go up another hundred yards and you will see the river. Get in and look around to acquaint yourself with the holes. You might as well wait on the bank until dark. Just yell if you need help landing a big one."

I said goodbye and walked down the trail. Like Larry said, in a hundred yards I could see the river.

The water looked black because of the dark river bottom and the tannic acid from the cedars and pines that had stained the water a deep tobacco color. The river was nearly one hundred feet wide and the current was slow. Weathered logs that looked like the dried bones of ancient creatures jutted from the water near the banks. Bright green shrubs and alders grew on the banks, softening the straight line of the water's edge. Fluffy blossoms covered their foliage like sprinkled white confetti. Behind the shrubs, tall cedars loomed above with a darker shade of green. Cedar waxwings fluttered on the branches, calling out excitedly in the heat. Somehow they must have known what was coming.

I walked down the bank and into the cool water. The drastic temperature change felt wonderful after the long hike. I held my hand in the slight current and brought some water to my face. It was deep here, almost too deep to wade, but I found my way to the center of the stream and located some holes that were well over six feet deep.

The largest of the holes was near several sunken logs, a perfect spot for large trout to lurk. The river bottom was a mixture of black muck and gravel. I walked upstream about a hundred feet and found an open area of soft grass as I waited for dusk.

Some of the rivers in Northern Michigan are blessed with one of the most spectacular mayfly hatches in the world. The robin may be our state bird, but on certain sections of large trout streams, the *Hexagenia limbata* is king. The mayfly's eggs hatch on the river bottom and the newly born nymphs live in the thick rich silt along the banks for up to two years. Then, with some inner clock that man has yet to understand, the mayflies emerge from their dark homes and drift to the surface. Their hard outer shell splits open in a grand metamorphosis. The mayfly rides the water, letting its wings dry and harden before taking to the air. The newly hatched flies then head for the foliage along the riverside, where they rest until nightfall of the next day. They always emerge at night, making this hatch all the more mysterious.

Because they are large, about the size of an anorexic humming-bird, the nymphs attract the largest trout in Michigan rivers. The German brown trout is a voracious night feeder, especially when it has reached bragging size. When trout reach a size where they are measured in pounds instead of inches, they feed mainly on other fish, frogs, crayfish, and the occasional mouse or other small animal that has the misfortune of falling into the river. The giant mayfly, hatching under cover of darkness, makes this one of the few times when wall-hanging browns can be caught on surface flies. Because of this, there is stiff competition among fishermen for the best holes.

I climbed the steep sandy bank on the opposite side of the river and sat between two thorn apple trees. Below me the dark river flowed silently in its journey to Lake Michigan. A slight breeze drifted from the west, bringing with it the tangy sent of the cedars and pines. Digging my wading shoes into the soft grass-covered sand, I shifted back and breathed deeply before preparing my rod. Yellow shafts of sunlight reached through the cedars and struck the water like golden spears as if trying to slow the sun's descent. A kingfisher glided past, coming to rest on a long-dead tree's smooth top branch. The bird looked over the water like a river keeper before crying out, proclaiming that all was in order. I expected the bird to fly on, but it did not. I watched the bird, feeling also like a river keeper.

With the light now fading, the sky turned from blue to a pastel green, still holding the shimmers of a hot summer's day. As night descended, pink and purple clouds formed on the horizon, some with sharp edges that ebbed into skyward mountain ranges stretching for hundreds of miles. Above me the clouds were ragged brush strokes, like splashes of watercolors slapped on the heavens by a mischievous boy. Coolness, like a heavy cloak, settled over the river, taking with it most of the intense heat, but leaving the humidity.

Cedar waxwings continued to call from the alders, along with grackles, as darkness came. I watched the birds skip from branch to branch as they waited impatiently for the upcoming feast. The first bats of the evening came out from hiding and circled the dark water in an airborne acrobatic performance. In the distance a whippoorwill sang, seeming to call the stars.

My reel clicked loudly in the stillness as I stripped off line and fed the leader through the guides of my rod. I straightened the leader and felt the smooth, stout monofilament between my fingers slowly taper until I reached the end of the tippet. The tippet material was heavier than I was used to, but necessary because of the large fly it must carry. Taking out my fly box, I selected a Hex pattern nearly the size of a sparrow and tied it snugly to the tippet. I coated the fly with dressing so it would ride high on the surface of the water. I checked the reel's drag then hooked the fly to the lower rod guide.

With the light now gone, the river looked like an ebony window that cut across the green meadowland. I stood slowly, feeling the stiffness in my legs from sitting for so long. Walking down the bank, I entered the river tentatively, feeling the coolness seep through my waders as the thin material clung to my legs. Another whippoorwill called, closer this time, its song flowing up the river like a greeting. I waded out farther, feeling my way across the slick gravel and over some submerged logs. The current pushed slowly at my belly when I reached the deep hole.

Above me the first stars appeared, straining to shine through the remaining light. Looking back to the water, I found it looked darker than moments before. I noticed a small cloud of mist to my right. Looking closer, I realized it was a hatch of tiny white insects that was so tightly packed over the river it looked like a gently moving ghost. Down the river more hatches of this type were occurring. Each was like a lightened spirit dancing over the water. I swept my hand through one of the clouds and caught a dozen of the tiny bugs, then watched as they returned to the undulating mist.

Lunar light broke through the top reaches of the cedars and spread across the water like a glistening glowing oil slick. I looked at the nearly full moon, its brightness making me squint. A trout rose in front of me with a gulp and a heavy splash. My eyes shot forward, watching as the rings reflected in the moonlight and spread outward into nothingness. A second rise followed, made by a smaller trout because it was splashy. In moments the air around me buzzed with life. A giant mayfly landed on my vest and I picked it up with my fingers. It was soft, moist, and full of life. The trout in front of me came up once more, just to my right and no more than twenty feet away. In moments the river seemed alive with feeding trout.

My hands shook as I released my fly and began laying out line for the first cast. The trout in front of me was feeding steadily now, with a gentle rhythm to his rise exactly twenty seconds apart. I timed my cast and tried to hit several feet above the last rise. I could not see my fly on the water. I waited nervously, holding my breath for the take. Nothing came. As I brought my rod back to pick up the line, he rose again, now to my left. Again and again I cast over him, each time sure that this would be the one.

The whippoorwill called again through the thick air. The huge trout was still feeding in front of me with the same rhythm. Now the air hummed with mayflies. In the moonlight I could see countless bodies floating down the river. I scooped my hand into the water and felt them as they bumped my fingers. Looking up the river, I could see hundreds of feeding trout. Some were fairly large rises, most were smaller, but none like the great fish in front of me. I had to have him.

I turned around and switched on a small flashlight attached to my vest. The sudden light blinded me for a moment, until my eyes adjusted to the beam. I pulled out my fly book and selected a similar but smaller pattern. As I tied on the fly, hundreds of mayflies swarmed to my vest, attracted by the light. They crawled on my arms, neck, and face as I quickly finished the tie. I could still hear the trout feeding with a heavy gulp and splash.

Captivated by the trout's behavior, I paused to study his actions. He was still feeding in twenty-second intervals. I began making false casts over him, waiting for another rise. He came up again, and I began to count. At fifteen I laid the line down and held my breath, seeing in my mind the drift of my fly. He rose again. Out of instinct I struck back and felt the heavy pulsating weight of a large fish. For a moment he remained still, as if confused, before thrusting forward toward the logs. I held the rod high and turned him away, trying to force him into the open water. He came back toward me, and I frantically pulled line to keep the connection tight. In front of me the water boiled, no more than five feet away. He shot past me, heading downstream, as the line screamed through my fingers then tightened on the reel. The drag began singing as more and more line escaped my reel. He was headed for another logjam. I held my rod high and tried to slow him. For a moment the line slowed, then stopped altogether. I could feel him far downstream, pulling against my rod.

Seconds passed without movement. I pumped the rod gently, trying to move him toward me, hoping to gain some line. He began to move now, slowly at first, fighting against the line and the dark current. I could feel every shake of his large head as he came to me like an old bull being led by a rope.

My line was moving cross-current, pulled by a trout with great strength in the black water. With the total darkness, I could only guess at his location by the direction of my rod and the small amount of fly line still wrapped on my reel. My rod tip pulsated and occasionally dipped quickly downward as he made another run. Minutes passed. I would gain some line, only to loose more moments later. The moon slipped behind a cloud and left me in total darkness, connected to a trout through a slender line.

Frantic heartbeats. This is what I will always remember most from the fight. Deep within my chest my heart was racing in anticipation of what I held. I imagined the trout's heart also pounding, unsure of his fate. For a few beautiful minutes we were blended together.

I was gaining line now. The trout moved back to his deep hole and made a few more small runs before reaching the surface in front of me. The clouds had passed and I could see him break the water in the moonlight. I reached behind and moved the net under the swirling shape, gently lifting and feeling the weight. He shook slowly in his woven cradle. He filled the net almost completely. Putting my rod under my arm and turning on my light, I saw him for the first time. The rich colors of the brown trout's spots were set against the rich golden sheen of his body. His large hooked jaw snapped out of instinct. Twenty-four inches, I guessed, give or take one or two, but at this point it did not matter. I held a trophy for which most fishermen can only dream. I removed the fly from his jaw and held the trout gently in my hands. Seconds later I lowered him back into the dark water and watched him swim free.

My hands were still shaking as I stood quietly, putting the memory of this great trout away. Across the river, more trout were rising, slurping the giant flies and splashing against the moonlight. I could hear the buzzing of the flies around me as they moved up and down the river. I closed my eyes to decide if I wanted to try for another trout or simply let the memory of this one end the evening.

Suddenly, high-intensity notes from an electric guitar startled me. Over the cedars and far beyond the swamp, someone was beginning to play. It was probably a garage band at a house that, until now, seemed miles away. Heavy deep notes came across the river like waves, echoing off the banks. I studied the music while watching the current turn silver under the moon as the mayflies hummed above me. The song was "Purple Haze," the one that made Hendrix famous. It brought back memories of my youth. I stood silently in the current, feeling the water and listening to the music. I wondered if it were possible to kiss the sky. Tonight, I decided, it was.

THIS CHILD

THE KINDERGARTEN TEACHER HAD USED ALL OF HER EDUCATIONAL leadership skills to arrange the class in the single-file line that now snaked slowly down the hallway. Because young children are easily distracted, the line undulated like a drunken serpent on a cold November day. Day-old ducklings follow their mother with more direction and attention than a kindergarten class on its way to the music room.

All I was trying to do was arrive at the principal's office without stepping over or on any of the little five-year-olds. This required a series of sidesteps and forced pauses as the little beings filed past me with curious looks and interested grins. I leaned against the cool cement block wall to wait my turn at open flooring, admiring the children's random wanderings. It was the last girl in line that boldly walked to my side.

She was no larger than the last trout I had pulled from Tutshi Lake in British Columbia. Her bright purple sweat suit was stained and baggy. It covered her from neck to toe, making her look like a giant dirty grape. Blond hair hung softly in her eyes, outlining a cheerful face and brilliant blue eyes. She stretched out her hand and took mine, gripping it tightly. She pulled me forward as she joined the other children. Not knowing exactly how to handle this situation, I followed obediently along, feeling her tiny fingers next to my rough skin.

I tried to remember her name as she led me proudly along the tiled floor toward the music room. Her teacher reached the door first and turned around to see that the newest and smallest pupil had found a rather large escort. "Thank you," the little girl said, pulling away from me and following the others inside the room. I found myself standing alone in the hallway looking at the confused teacher with nothing to say.

It was nearly two weeks later when I saw her again. Her class, along with hordes of other youngsters, was packed tightly in the cafeteria for lunch. Somehow she saw me walk through the maze of colorful tables and the whirlwind of activity that is customary for a primary school lunchroom. As I stood there, surrounded by the din of a hundred full mouths and giggling voices, she walked up and took my hand. She squeezed it firmly and looked innocently into my eyes. I was embarrassed at first, or at least somewhat self-conscious, but that soon gave way to wonder. *Why was this child singling me out among the other adults in the building?* It took a combination of cotton candy and a spilled glass of punch to answer this question.

Each spring the Clare Primary School holds an annual carnival, dedicated to providing the young students with an opportunity to consume gigantic quantities of sweets and participate in a large array of games of chance. The event is widely publicized for fundraising and provides an opportunity for parents to learn about the school and to brag about their children. I attended this event more for public relations reasons than school security. The building was filled, nearly overflowing with energetic children and tired-looking adults. Volunteers managed various games in the hallways and gymnasium, hoping to attract the wandering throng of interested participants. The cafeteria held the refreshment stands, complete with all sorts of calorie-laden items. I took a glass of sweet punch and settled against the gray cement block wall to watch the crowd.

Across the room one of the more aggressive students was selling cotton candy with a flair only possible in the early grades. He held each pile of spun sugar in front of him like a mighty sword, ready to joust with each passing parent and child. I admired his enthusiasm and dedication to fundraising enough to momentarily forget my perpetual diet.

"Officer White," he said, pushing a large cone of pink fluff in my direction. "Want some cotton candy?"

I paid the dollar and took the sticky gift from his stickier hand, before retreating backward to an open area of the room. What I didn't know was that a chair had been pushed in my path of retreat. I stumbled back and luckily managed to keep from falling onto a table, which is more than I can say for my Styrofoam cup of punch. The combination of Sprite and ruby-red Kool-Aid fell to the floor and oozed around the scrambling feet of at least a dozen children of assorted ages. A chorus of giggles and a half-hearted round of applause followed, as I unintentionally became the center of attention. I made apologies to all the people around me, then sat on a long bench while a school custodian began the mopping up process. The custodian held a large pile of paper towels and smeared the pink mixture over the white tile, all the while grinning in my direction. He was on his third fist-full when I saw her approach.

The little girl came prancing through the crowd. She had several crumpled tissues which, apparently, she had taken from her pocket. She glanced in my direction then got on her knees to help the custodian with the punch pick up. I marveled at her effort and the obvious fact that she was doing this for me. When her tissues were nearly the color of my stick of cotton candy, she rose and walked toward me. She carefully set the tissues on the bench and sat down. She smiled up into my eyes and took my hand in hers.

"What is your name?" I asked.

Her mouth formed a crooked grin as she proudly said, "Hannah." She squeezed my hand tightly and brought it to her lap before looking back at my face. "My name is spelled the same backwards and forwards," she said.

I laughed out loud at her statement. "It certainly is, Hannah. You have a wonderful name. Are you here with your parents?"

Hannah's smile disappeared. She looked embarrassed. Her eyes fell downward to our entwined hands. She put her other hand over mine and softly spoke. "My mom dropped me off. She has to work a lot. I don't have a dad. I don't know what it is like to have a dad." She squeezed my hand again and looked up at me, nearly in tears. "I'll bet you're a good dad," she said quietly.

Seventeen years of police training and over three decades of life experience had not prepared me for this. I realized that I was a thirty-six-year-old man who did not know how to respond. I looked down at our intertwined hands and at the tiny being that wished her life was different. Suddenly I felt a kinship with Hannah. The pain of innocence and the wonder of hope overcame me in that hot crowded cafeteria. We sat silently for several minutes, each watching the fathers, mothers, and children moving through the room. I cleared my throat and looked down at this child.

"Hannah, would you like to hang out with me tonight?" I asked, tears forming in my eyes. She looked up at me with a smile as I handed her the cotton candy.

CALVIN

I NEVER GAVE MUCH THOUGHT TO CALVIN. HE WAS JUST THE PAUNCHY kid who worked at an out- of-the-way convenience store, waiting on people who were on their way to somewhere else. His hair was generally unkempt and his clothes were always rumpled, making him look like someone who set the alarm clock only minutes before work time. I knew his name only from the crooked patch on his gray work shirt. I had no idea of his shift schedule, but he always seemed to be working each time I stopped at the store on my way to somewhere else.

Whenever I could arrange a brief hiatus from police work, I liked to drive north to the upper reaches of a blue-ribbon trout stream that happened to be only a few miles from Calvin's store. Sitting at the intersection of two county roads, which had heavy traffic before the expressway was opened, the store looked a little run down, but the beverages were cold. It became my regular stop before stepping in the river.

Usually I would pull into the dusty parking lot late in the after-noon and grab a few items for the evening. Calvin would be sitting behind the counter on an old, battered stool, either reading a maga-zine or just staring at the beer posters that lined the dirty walls. The buttons on his shirt would strain against his protruding belly as he stood to adjust his sagging pants. As I walked to the rear of the store toward the coolers, he would say "How ya doin?" I always replied, but more out of courtesy than real interest.

Sometimes Calvin would attempt a conversation during our brief transaction at the cash register. He was always polite, but he never made eye contact. I assumed that he had poor self-esteem. He made comments about the weather, the upcoming season of the Detroit Lions, or current road conditions. Calvin never mentioned fishing, even though he worked within a few minutes of several famous trout rivers. I was not surprised because he did not appear to be someone who would understand the beauty of mayflies and jumping trout. I would have talked more with him, but I just assumed that there was nothing he and I had in common.

One day, near the end of my drive north, I realized that I had forgotten to pick up a spool of 6X tippet material. With no fly shops nearby, and knowing that Calvin's store only carried a few bait fishing supplies, I considered driving another thirty miles, but I pulled into the dusty parking lot just in case. Calvin was behind the counter reading an off-road magazine. He greeted me as usual. I said hello and walked to the far corner, where there were a few old bait casting rods hung on the dirty wall. I looked at everything on the rack, finding nothing remotely close to tippet material.

"Looking for something?" Calvin yelled from the counter.

"Yeah, but you don't carry it," I replied with disappointment.

"What do you need?"

"Some tippet material," I said, not expecting him to know what it was.

"What size?"

"Oh, 6X," I said, already giving up hope and eyeing the cold sodas in the case.

"Got a spool in my car. I will sell it to you."

I almost replied, *you're kidding*, but caught myself. "Sure, if you can spare it."

"Here, watch the counter and I will be right back," he said.

Calvin was smiling as he lumbered out the door toward the old Chevy Nova parked at the end of the lot. I expected him to return with a roll of six-pound test, and was already planning on how to explain the difference to him, when he came back with a nearly full spool of 6X. It was the same brand that I used.

"Here, mister," he said, handing me the spool. "You come up all these times to fly fish?"

"Yes," I replied. "Are you a fly fisherman?"

Calvin stared at the floor, digging his toe into a slightly exposed nail. "Yeah, my granddaddy taught me. I go every chance I get."

"Me, too," I said, pulling out my wallet. "Know some good places around here?" I asked, handing him the money.

"Just the ones granddad showed me," he said, walking behind the counter.

I thanked him for the tippet material and walked out of the store. I sat in my car for several minutes looking at the tippet material and feeling a little guilty. For all these years I had treated Calvin as a non-person; someone that was not capable of enjoying the same level of fishing as me. I remembered the smile and eagerness on his face as he ran out to his battered car to give me something that I needed and, in a way, something we both shared.

I walked back into the store and up to the counter. Calvin was thumbing through the magazine. "What time do you get off work today, Calvin?" I asked. His face lit up, as if I had just handed him a one-hundred dollar bill.

"My boss takes over in about an hour. I go home after that."

"Would you like to go fishing with me tonight?"

"Sure," he said, staring down at the counter. "I have my stuff in my car. And I know a really good place."

"That's okay, Calvin," I said. "I'm not asking to find out your secret spots. You can go with me."

"That's okay. I *want* to take you to my favorite spot. You'll like it."

"Okay," I said. "Where do we meet?"

"You know where Ridge Road crosses Singing Creek?"

"Sure, but the creek is awfully small."

"Just meet me there," Calvin said, rearranging some papers on the counter. "You'll like this spot."

I left the store and drove around for a while. I went to the bridge and sat listening to the radio, thinking about fishing with Calvin. I would help him. I could show him some of fly fishing's finer techniques and maybe give him a few flies. What could it hurt? I got out of the car and looked at the creek. It was only about ankle deep and appeared impossible to fish. Nearly an hour passed, and I began putting on my gear. I had just finished lacing up my wading shoes when I heard the rumble of the old Nova coming up the road.

Calvin roared to a stop and sort of rolled from the car. "You sure there are trout in this creek?" I asked, as he went around to the trunk.

"Not in the creek. You'll see," he said. "You'll see."

Calvin put on a battered plaid shirt and picked up an ancient bamboo fly rod. He walked toward me and smiled. "Ready to go?" he asked.

"Yes. Do you have everything?"

"All here," he said, patting the several bulges in his shirt pockets. "Just follow me," he said as he stepped into the ditch.

I followed Calvin closely. There was a faint path that followed the creek. It appeared to be nothing more than a deer trail. I was working up quite a sweat and wondering where this would finally end. Soon we entered a cedar swamp and were climbing over stumps and roots. "How much farther?" I asked, not wanting to seem impatient.

"Almost there," he replied.

Soon I could hear the river. I had no idea it swung this far toward the road. Moments later I saw it. We walked up to the bank. Before me lay a beautiful sight; a wide stretch of blue-ribbon trout stream that in all my years of fishing here, I had no idea existed.

I looked over the river and could already see an occasional rise. I stepped in and sat on an old log along the bank. I heard Calvin get in and watched as he pieced together his rod. He wore no waders and was ready to fish in what seemed like seconds. I could tell he was waiting for me. "What fly are you starting with?" I asked, as I strung my leader through the guides of my rod.

"Lots of hoppers and crickets around. I tied on one of these."

I looked at the fly. It was a brown deer hair body with lots of hackle and deer hair for a wing.

"Sort of looks like a hopper or something, don't it?" Calvin asked. "It always catches fish around here. What you using?" he asked, staring at my graphite rod.

"I think I will start with a Royal Wolf," I said, "It always seems to catch fish for me."

"Don't look much like a bug, but if it works, it works," he said.

"Go ahead and fish Calvin. It will take me a while here," I said, struggling with my fly line.

"Okay," he said walking out into the center of the river.

I watched as he worked his way toward a logjam. I went back to setting up my rod and straightening out the leader. I figured I would let him fish for a while, then offer some tips. None were needed.

The only way to describe Calvin's casting was to say that he became one with the rod. He stripped off some line and paused, looking upstream to the eddy behind a logjam. *He cannot possibly cast that far*, I thought. I was wrong.

The river was too deep for him to wade further and he was looking at about a sixty-foot cast. At least. Calvin studied the braided current like a mountain climber about to plan the best route. With a sudden flash the rod was brought forward, pulling the line from the water in back of him into a sharp strike as it straightened in the evening air. Back the rod moved, bent under the pressure then forward again, as he released more line. After five or six false casts he had nearly sixty feet of bright line in the air. It sailed above him in a perfect loop with tiny droplets of water falling around him in the evening light. I was so enamored with his skill that I almost missed the final cast. The fly settled behind the jam in the back of the eddy and hung there motionless for several seconds before disappearing. Calvin struck gently, poetically. His rod bent under the heavy pull. That was the moment I learned not to judge people by appearances.

The large brown trout jumped twice before staying down and fighting against the line. Calvin worked the trout like a master, giving line, taking line, never appearing rattled or even concerned. After about three minutes the trout was cradled in his landing net. He was removing the hook as I walked to his side.

"Well done," I said, looking at the fifteen-inch fish bright with color.

"Thanks," he answered, dropping the net and letting the fish return to his eddy. "My granddad always said to release the better fish. It makes the stream healthy." He dried his fly and hooked it on the cork handle of his rod. "I learned a lot from my granddad," he said quietly.

I had, too.

SCARY THINGS

IT IS NO SECRET THAT I DON'T LIKE SPIDERS. OKAY, PERHAPS IT IS A secret to the world at large, but not to my close friends who, after many years of friendship, have become quite sympathetic when I happen to have one of the nasty things crawling on my neck. By *sympathetic* I mean they don't drop completely to their knees with laughter, they just bend over at the waist and hold their shaking bellies. Not that I have anything personal against the disgusting little arachnids. It's the disgusting *big* arachnids that I have a problem with, particularly the large, brown, hairy, fang-snapping, flesh-eating ones that seem to think that crawling on my neck is some kind of sport. Having a grand dislike for spiders is especially unfortunate for me because of my love of fly fishing.

Time spent along the blue-ribbon trout streams of northern Michigan is one of my favorite pastimes. Unfortunately, the streamside alders are usually crawling with spiders. Because of the large insect hatches that make fishing with flies so successful, the local hairy things have a bountiful smorgasbord along the rivers. This, of course, presents several problems for a true arachniofobic. Because I have a habit of tangling my line within these branches, I am constantly faced with spider encounters. As soon as my line is tangled in an alder, I scan the foliage for any approaching crawlers. The

81

problem is not that I *think* the spiders are actually trying to attack me, it's that I *know* the spiders are trying to attack me. There have been many times when one of my best flies became wrapped around a limb in a kind of streamside macramé design, and I just snapped it off rather than reach in among the creepy things. This dilemma is solved when I fish with my friend Ken. Aside from being a good friend and fine fly fisherman, Ken has no fear of spiders, which makes him, as far as I am concerned, the perfect fishing companion. Over the years Ken has learned that when I tangle up, he must retrieve my fly. It still amazes me how he can reach into the brush for my fly as spiders dance among the branches and over his bare arms. The logs, however, present other problems.

The better trout streams of Michigan are littered with logs that simply beg to be sat upon. One of my favorite parts of fly fishing is to contemplate the many aspects of life while sitting on an old log. The problem is that these logs are often home to the alder-dweller's larger cousins. Ken, being the good friend he is, always checks each log for any eight-legged occupanct. Always gentle with his approach to my phobia, hearing Ken clear his throat and shake his head back and forth tells me that this particular log is already inhabited. While having no fear of spiders, Ken does have a fear of his own. Ken fears snakes.

Ken's loathing of the long reptiles is at least equal to, or even greater than, my fear of spiders. Many times while walking to our favorite stretch of river I will see Ken lock up like a prized bird dog on point. Knowing that a snake is in the path, I will advance forward to remove or guard against the scaly thing. Because I have no fear of snakes and Ken has no fear of spiders, we make a terrific fly fishing team.

One of the things that Ken and I have discussed at great length is the frequency in which we each encounter the source of our fears. It seems to always be Ken who stumbles upon the snakes. While I can spend days in the woodlands of Michigan and never see one of the forked-tongued reptiles, Ken is constantly tripping over them. On the other hand, it seems to always be me who encounters, up close and personal, the largest and scariest of spiders. I once discussed this phenomenon with a local psychologist who assured me that the frequency of our encounters only *seems* to be at a higher rate because of our phobia. He stated that because of our fears, we give each of these occurrences greater weight, therefore creating the *illusion* that the objects in question are appearing more frequently. Of course, Ken and I know in our hearts that he is wrong.

Central Michigan trout streams are the breeding and stalking grounds for a particular species of spider that spends most of its day on old gray logs in and along rivers. Because of its size, I suspect they are waiting to attack a passing meal, like a squirrel or a small deer. These things are huge. With no exaggeration, I have seen some the size of my hand—and with more hair. Simply wading past one of these giants is sometimes enough to drive me from the stream. What bothers me more than just seeing one is the indisputable fact that it has to have a mother and father and, more than likely, brothers and sisters. These spiders come in a variety of colors, but death-brown is the most common. I suspect that some wildlife biologist could tell me their exact species, but who really cares.

One day I was fishing a lovely little stream called Newton Creek just north of Clare. I had just made a grand cast that resulted in my fly being tangled in some brush. The particular limb that snagged my fly was resting against a rather large log. As I pumped my rod and walked forward in an attempt to dislodge the fly, I noticed one of the before-mentioned hairy giants. The limb shot back in place, knocking the spider into the watery current. At first I was pleased. *Hah*, I thought. *Looks like Mr. log dweller gets to take a little swim.* Before I could further congratulate myself on causing an inconvenience to one of my arch nemeses, I realized this nemesis would float right past me. This presented several problems, the most serious of which was that I couldn't move away fast enough in the heavy muck of the river bottom.

As the spider drifted by, I realized that it was one of the largest I had ever seen. It clung to the surface like an eight-legged cat ready to pounce. I got chills as it drifted within two feet of my legs. I could actually see the large fangs on its evil head. To explain what happened next, I will give a brief study in the survival instincts of large river spiders. This will serve the reader with an understanding of why the spider reacted the way it did and why I have an annoying twitch whenever I am near a river log.

When resting on a streamside log waiting for a passing meal, like a stray dog or a fisherman, spiders require some type of overhead cover to protect them from detection and predation from birds of prey, such as great blue herons, giant eagles, or low-flying fighter jets. This explains why this particular spider was under the fly catching branch. On the water, however, the spider was vulnerable to hunters from above as well as large fish, such as a great white shark, from below. Simply stated, an exposed spider on the water needs to find cover as quickly as possible. You can understand, then, why this spider would pick the closest object to climb on.

For the next portion of our lesson, the reader must understand that a spider has wonderful vision, but only up close. Thus, it must rely on its sense of feel for objects farther away, like movements of a large web, or in my case, the stream's current. Through evolution, the spider has learned that objects sticking out of a river cast a break in the current. This can be demonstrated by sticking a tree limb in an area of flat current and seeing the neat V that is formed downstream. Although a spider has a relatively small brain, it does know that if it follows such a V wake it will eventually find an out-of-the-water object. Unfortunately for me, the only thing breaking the current and making the great V of safety were my legs. I will now continue with the incident.

The fang-snapping flesh-eating spider drifted motionlessly down the slick flat water past me. Although I was shaking and beginning to perspire like a fat man in a sauna, I thought I was safe. And I was—until it hit the V formed by my legs. It felt this indicator of refuge about ten feet downstream and, like a dehydrated man crawling desperately toward an oasis, began scampering up the V current. My initial thought was to pull out my service weapon and fill the spider with several rounds of hollow-point ammunition. The only problem was that I had left my gun at home. So I did the next best thing, which was to back up quickly, attempting to out- distance the beast. Because of the mucky bottom, I could not move fast enough away from my greatest fear. Besides, a huge spider can move quickly on the water when it is in danger.

Seeing that speed was on the spider's side, I tried to slap at the evil thing with my rod tip. At this point I remembered that I was still hung up on the limb and the rod would not reach the water, let alone the approaching fang-snapper. Instead of striking the approaching spider, I merely waved the rod over his head, like a conductor directing his scampering movements. "Flight of the Bumble Bee" would have been an appropriate soundtrack.

I quickly calculated the rate of gain of the approaching monster and found I had only seconds left before contact. I thought of the headlines in the local paper: *Award-winning police officer and local author dies after wrestling match with giant spider.*

When the creature was about a foot from my leg, I dropped my rod into the water and began splashing frantically, trying to move enough water so it would drown, or at least go away. Unfortunately, my spider took this as a challenge. I was moving water like an unruly child in a neighborhood swimming pool, but the thing was going nowhere. In fact, the spider seemed to enjoy the challenge, riding the waves like a hairy California surfer on steroids. I thought I heard it say "Cool Dude."

Finally, with a push from my hands made possible with a huge adrenaline rush, I drove forward with so much force that I almost touched the evil being. The resulting mini tidal wave dunked the spider under the water, where it floundered for a few seconds, then surfaced a foot or so downstream. I could see its awful glare as it studied me for signs of weakness. It would have seen many, but decided to give up on this particular point of refuge. To my relief, it drifted downstream and around the bend.

When my heart slowed to panic level, I removed my fly from the branch after checking for spider relatives. I was shaking so badly that I decided to end this fishing trip and go home to sit around in a cold sweat. It wasn't until several miles away that I had an even scarier thought. *What if I didn't see the spider hit the water?* I would have continued fishing upstream as the thing crawled up the back of my leg. To this day that thought haunts me.

Later in the year, when I had enough composure to fish once more and Ken and I were together on the stream, I told him of the incident. Ken, being the kind and understanding friend that he is, only held his hands over his face while he laughed. When I calmly explained that the same thing could happen with a snake, he stopped.

TWO IN THE NIGHT

LARRY WAITED PATIENTLY BY THE FRONT OF MY TRUCK AS I FINISHED tying on the fly. He leaned against the fender and looked back at the forest like an experienced guide waiting for his green-horn client to quit fumbling around. With the help of my pen-sized flashlight I finished attaching the giant fly, which was larger than a hummingbird, to the heavy tippet. Moments later I closed the tailgate with let's-go authority.

Darkness enveloped the tiny meadow on this hot sticky night. Normally this was the time of day when fishing ends, not begins, but I was excited to try casting after dark in search of large trout. Large brown trout are mostly nocturnal. They patrol the deeper pools in the darkness, taking nearly anything that can be a meal. Large trout will eat mice, frogs, or even ducklings.

I walked to Larry's side and waited for his direction. He said nothing but began moving cautiously through the thick alders that bordered the river. The swampy ground moved with each footstep, at times sinking several inches before springing back as my weight shifted. The thickness of the foliage compounded the difficulty of the hike as wispy branches and tall grass slapped against my body in the darkness. It was like trying to walk on a trampoline suspended in a thick Peruvian jungle.

Total darkness surrounded us, with only the bright nearly full moon and a smattering of stars giving some light. In the distance a whippoorwill called out hauntingly, backed up by a chorus of frogs. Being in a swamp is always a little scary (although most adults will never admit this fact). Something about dark wet places holds a certain mysterious quality around what is unseen. A dark night compounds these foreboding feelings to the point of goose bumps and quick glances to the rear. I followed along, wondering exactly why I was here and hoping that I would not get lost. I was comforted by having an experienced friend and guide who, among other things, did not seem the least bit frightened.

Larry was about ten feet in front of me. I could hear him moving through the brush. I was amazed that he could find the river in this maze of alders. I stopped and listened for river sounds, but could hear nothing but his footsteps in the swamp. A few steps further I became tangled in some sort of root and fell hard against the damp ground. Larry did not hear the dull thud and continued moving ahead of me. I scrambled to my feet and rushed to catch up, plowing through the brush like a wader-clad bigfoot. Moments later I reached Larry. He was standing at the river's edge, outlined against the moonlight-bathed water. His arms were folded with his rod held close to his body like an infantryman holding a rifle.

"We'll start here, then work upstream," Larry said, his voice sounding strange after the long walk in silence. "There are several good holes in this section." He eased into the river and walked several feet to center stream.

I followed behind, enjoying the feel of the cold water through my waders. Larry was only a dark silhouette against the water. I could sense the current pushing against my legs, indicating upstream from down, but the moon and stars and their reflection on the water were the only source of light. I looked around and could not see either bank, let alone what lay ahead. Were it not for the dim moonlight, this would be like spending time in one of those sensory- deprivation chambers. Larry began moving again and I did my best to keep up. Each step was somewhat dangerous, as I could see nothing in the water. The bottom was sandy, but also covered in decaying branches and other assorted river land mines, making my wading a game of step, shuffle, and pray. To compound matters, the streamside plant life, mainly consisting of alders and the occasional cedar, branched out, so to speak, over the river at about neck-level. These obstacles were invisible and only located when they struck my face. Knowing that these outgrowths were literally crawling with spiders did nothing to add pleasantness to this adventure. Because I am a long-time arachnophobic, the thought of the eight-legged beings having such easy access to my body caused much concern. Pulling sticky webs from my sweating face was terrible, especially when the actual creators couldn't be seen.

Larry stopped in a section of shallow water and waited for me. I was still pulling off webs and swatting imaginary crawlers when I reached his side. "I'll let you have the first hole," Larry said with a whisper. "Cast straight upstream and listen for a strike."

"Say, Larry," I said, looking into the blackness. "How will I know if my fly hits the water or brush?"

"You won't at first. Wait and feel for your line drifting back. If you hear a splash, set the hook."

I stripped off some line and began false-casting. I could see nothing straight on, but peripherally I could almost make out the streamside brush. Overhead I could hear the huge fly whistling in the heavy air, sounding like a fluttering bat. I stopped my rod and felt the line fall forward. Silence followed as I stared into the blackness slowly stripping line and guessing the current speed. My line became tight and I struck hard. Larry laughed hard and took a step forward.

"You hooked the brush on the far side," he said. He followed my line into the trees and pulled down my fly. "Let's try the next hole," he said, moving on upstream.

The next two holes were the same. Not being able to see anything, I continued to cast my fly onto everything *but* the water. We worked up to a spot Larry called his honey hole. "I always take a nice trout from this place," he said with excitement.

I really wanted to catch a trout—not so much for my own enjoyment, but to please Larry. I felt the current against my legs and tried to gauge its speed. I wished that I could see more than black empty space before me. It was at this point that I remembered the man and his blind daughter at the Bambi movie.

"Ah . . . Larry," I said. "You've fished this hole in the daylight . . . right?"

"Sure, lots of times."

"And even in the dark, you know exactly where we are in relation to the brush and the deepest part of the hole and the overhanging trees and such?"

"Yes."

I closed my eyes. "I want you to describe this spot. Not in a general sense, but in minute detail. Start with the width of the river and the current speed, then the distances in relation to the brush and trees. I want you to pretend that I am blind and you are painting this place in my mind, like a picture." Larry was quiet for a moment, then understood my plan.

"You are standing in the center of the stream. You have about eight feet on either side, approximately the length of your rod. For ten feet straight ahead, the stream bottom is level and the flow equal to what you feel on your legs. Above that, the stream makes a gradual dogleg to the left on about a thirty-degree angle. At the apex of the curve, the water slows and is about three feet deep. Five feet above the apex is the hole. The deepest part is near the bank. The water over the hole moves very slowly in a clockwise manner.

My eyes remained closed. From Larry's voice I could now clearly see the stream. "Okay, now fill in the brush and trees."

"On the right bank, all the way around the curve, are alders. Their branches stop at the water's edge except for one that hangs over about two feet just upstream from the hole. To your left are more alders until the stream begins to curve. At the start of the curve is a short cedar tree that hangs over the water about six feet. Just above the cedar is a small logjam that directs the current toward the hole. You need to cast above the logjam and nearly under the overhanging alder. Your fly should then drift over the hole."

I smiled. I could clearly see the scene in my mind. To my surprise, this vision continued as I began false casting. I could actually see my line and the attached fly flowing through the air. I could see my target and was able, I thought, to accurately judge the distance. I held my eyes tightly closed and made the cast, seeing the fly settle just above the overhanging alders and move over the deep hole. Suddenly there was a splash. It may be hard to believe, but I actually saw the strike in my mind. Out of instinct, my rod shot back to set the hook.

The trout was not large, by most standards, but big enough to put up a fine fight. With my eyes still closed, I played the fish and tried to keep it from the logjam. After about one minute the fish was nearly at my side. I opened my eyes to the blackness and Larry landed the trout in his net with the aid of a small flashlight. At nearly sixteen inches, it was indeed a fine trout.

"It must have worked well," Larry said, holding up the net and grinning in the flashlight's yellow glow.

I released the fish and looked at the blackness in front of me. Closing my eyes I once again saw the lovely hole where the fish lived. "I think I am going to like this night fishing," I said.

PEACHES

S HE LAY CONTENTEDLY IN THE PATCHWORK OF SHADE BENEATH THE alders, looking more like a lawn ornament than a small white-tail doe. The thick green grass and lace-like ferns that surrounded the deer were in deep contrast to her reddish summer coat. A gentle breeze tossed the foliage, splashing her with sunlight in the warm, bright summer afternoon. She raised her nose slightly, trying to separate our scent from the rich earthy smell of the meadow and the sweet odor of the tall ferns. Behind the doe the river tumbled over a gravel bottom creating a musical backdrop. It was the deer's expression that I found unusual. A timid animal this close to humans would normally be in a panic, or at least deeply concerned, but she held a look of total relaxation, bordering on amusement. She rested confidently in her soft green bed, like a young lady who wondered what the silly boys would do.

Mark pulled out his camera from the glove box and took several small steps forward before reaching the fence. I expected the doe to bolt into the deep brush at the movement, but she remained calm, only her ears becoming alert with his approach. After several photographs Mark moved closer and leaned against the wire fence. "She must have a fawn hidden in there," he said quietly.

"Or she's sick or injured," Ken said, walking to Mark's side. He moved his fly rod over the fence and waved it slowly only a few feet from the deer's nose. The little doe followed the rod's movement with her nose, sniffing it with interest. "Let's tell everyone that I hypnotized her," Ken laughed.

"I'll take a look," I said, slowly climbing over the fence. The deer watched intently as I cautiously moved ahead several feet. "Hi there, little one," I whispered, holding my hand only three feet from her nose. She stood slowly like a tired dog. She took a few steps toward the river. "I can't see anything wrong. She looks healthy enough," I said over my shoulder toward my friends. I pulled a handful of thick grass and extended the bunch toward her. To my surprise the deer stepped daintily forward and pulled about half the grass from my hand and began munching. I ran my hand over her slender neck, feeling the soft slick hair. She took the rest of the grass without hesitation.

"I wouldn't touch her," Ken said with concern. His paramedic training and years of medical experience made him cautious of potential diseases.

I moved to her side and ran my hands along her back feeling the hard ridge of her spine. She moved closer, leaning toward my soft touch. My hands felt her rib cage down to the softness of her abdomen. Dropping to my knees, I was nearly at eye level with her slender face and shiny nose. She stepped closer and smelled my fishing vest, going from pocket to pocket, taking in the strange odors. Her eyes were clear and bright and looked at me like a companion rather than a threat.

"Don't you wish all women were that easy?" Mark chuckled. He began climbing over the fence to meet my new girlfriend.

"Ken, do you have your stethoscope with you?" I asked without looking from the deer.

"Yeah, I have one in the truck. Just a second." Ken walked to the truck cab and grabbed his medical kit.

Mark stood on the other side of the deer, petting her like a friendly dog. "What are we going to name her?" he asked, moving his hands to playfully rub her ears.

"Peaches," Ken said, climbing over the fence and walking up next to me. He opened his kit and put on a pair of rubber exam gloves.

"Peaches," Mark said with a grin. "Why Peaches?"

"Oh, I don't know. She just looks like a deer you would call Peaches. You boys have any other suggestions?"

"Peaches it is," I said, moving back so Ken could begin his examination.

Ken moved the stethoscope pad behind the deer's front shoulder and listened intently with the professional worry of a trained medic. He moved the pad to her other side, thrusting his hand underneath the deer. "Lungs sound clear. I was worried about tuberculosis or some other respiratory infection. The DNR reported that some deer have been infected with TB in this area." He took off his scope and took the deer's head in his gloved hands. Opening her mouth, he looked inside, before turning his attention to her nostrils. Ken stood and began feeling under her jaw. "No gland enlargement," he said. He moved down her neck to her chest before turning around and pushing on her belly. I watched intently as Ken continued his professional examination.

"Say, Ken," I said loudly, while looking at Mark. "If this stream-bank exam requires a pelvic, Mark and I can go wait by the river. You bring stirrups with you?"

"Yeah, we won't tell a soul," Mark said with a smile.

Ken grinned and stood, rubbing the doe behind her ear like a pet dog. "I pronounce her healthy," he said. "The little girl must have been raised by someone since she was a fawn. Probably dropped her off here this summer."

"Well, gentlemen," Mark said in his best leadership voice. "Now that we have solved the great Bambi mystery, perhaps it is time for a little fishing adventure."

We left Peaches at her spot under the alders and trudged to the river. By the bridge the stream was only calf deep, flowing rapidly into the dark steep hills and thick swampy brush. Walking down-stream about a hundred feet, we left behind the bridge crossing and other signs of human development. Our plan was to walk down with the river's flow for about a mile, then fish back upstream for the rest of the day. As we walked, the river narrowed and deepened and became the classic pool-riffle combination that made this a fine fish-ery. By the second bend Mark and Ken were several yards ahead of me. I too was anxious to fish, but I always tended to go slowly on these excursions, enjoying the wonder of an early summer day on a fine trout stream.

With the water now waist deep, it was like walking in a moving channel of life through a deep-green world. The river was boarded on each side with towering cedars and lush alders that stood like guardians of pleasure and warning. Sunlight pushed through the trees and turned the water to sparkling patterns, exaggerating the deep recesses of shade. I knew that the deep pockets contained trout, but, like Ken and Mark, I forced myself to refrain from fishing until we reached our chosen destination. Sometimes fishing like this is a lesson in restraint.

I heard something behind me and turned around quickly. "Hey, guys," I shouted over the gentle wind and river noise. Mark and Ken turned and looked at me with surprised faces. I looked back at them, pointing my thumb over my shoulder. "We have a guest today," I said, shaking my head.

Peaches pranced along the river, keeping to the shallow water by the bank. She ran past, splashing me and running right up to Ken. "Interesting doctor-patient relationship," Mark said. "You obviously made quite an impression on our cloven-hoofed friend."

Ken held out his hand and let Peaches smell his fingers. "You want to go fishing little one?" he asked while rubbing her neck.

"No one is going to believe this," Mark said, taking out his camera and shooting several shots. When the roll was finished, he put it away and began walking back downstream.

I followed along, watching as Ken and his new friend tagged behind. Peaches did not always stay by Ken's side, but it was obvious that she had chosen him over Mark and me. She would run across the river at shallow areas, playing in the thin water with joy. In the deep areas she could go out on the bank, sometimes leaving our sight before running ahead and waiting for Ken to catch up. When we reached our spot to begin fishing, we separated, each of us taking a good section of water. Peaches stayed near Ken, just downstream from me. For his part, Ken was quite patient with his new companion. This was important because Peaches was more than an interesting novelty on the river.

"Hey," Ken yelled, breaking me from my current trance of fly casting. I looked down the stream to find Ken and Peaches in a tug-of-war with his landing net. She had the net firmly in her mouth, pulling Ken toward the bank. I could hear him laugh as he struggled to pull it free. The last I saw of the two of them before I moved out of their sight was Ken sitting on the bank while Peaches splashed around in his fishing hole.

At the end of the evening we walked out of the river with Peaches by Ken's side. We left her to her little grove by the road and went back to camp, each wondering if she would be there in the morning. We need not have worried.

For the next two mornings of our fishing trip, Peaches greeted us at the bridge, walking confidently to Mark's truck and waiting for attention. Ken brought some apples from camp and fed her slices he had carved with his pocketknife. Mark and I watched and grinned as Ken fed the little deer like an eager puppy that nudged his elbow when he was not fast enough.

Peaches fished with us each day, sometimes wading in the river, other times prancing around on the shore, but always within sight of Ken. She would watch him make long casts over the pools and rif-fles and would often run down to his side while he played a trout. Ken would take the fish from the hook and hold it to her nose before releasing it back into the water. Mark and I did experience a little jealousy from Ken's new relationship, but it was fairly short-lived when we saw how much fishing time Ken lost because of her antics.

On our last night on the river we returned to the old bridge, wish-ing that more time could be spent on this fine trout stream. We watched the river with tired satisfaction as the last light of day faded into blackness and the night sounds of whippoorwills and crickets filled the absence of daylight. Mark and I put our gear into his truck and shed our waders for the short trip back to camp. Ken stood by the fence rubbing Peaches on her neck, talking softly.

"And remember," he said in a whisper. "Don't stay by the road all the time. Not all people are like us. Some people are bad and you should hide in the alders until dark." Ken looked back toward us with a smile. "Be careful of the bucks, too," he said sternly. "They only want one thing. There is nothing wrong with being single for a season or two."

Peaches stood in the thick grass by the road and watched us get into the truck. Beyond the little deer, the dark hills faded from rich green to black as the coolness of a summer night descended like a heavy blanket of peace. The last thing I saw that night was the full moon rising over the black hills.

It was several weeks before we returned to the river. We parked by the old bridge and hopped out of Mark's truck, searching for Peaches. Ken climbed over the fence and looked for the deer hope-fully. "Peaches!" he shouted toward the deep brush. At first there was nothing, just the deep green of the foliage and the rich smell of late summer. Then, out she came, prancing from the alders with that happy look we all loved. She went to Ken first, of course, then to each of us. We rubbed her sides and fed Peaches the apples and carrots Ken had brought for her. She spent the next two afternoons with a very relieved Ken along the river.

In September the aspens turned to a golden patchwork on the rolling hills. Sugar maples and dogwood shone like a crimson explosion, turning the countryside into a mosaic of color. The river flowed clear and cold in the crisp morning, sending a thin fog up the rich cedars along the banks. It would be our last trout fishing trip of the season, although we wished there could be more. Winter was fast approaching, and we looked on this last trip fondly. Ken paused before getting out of the truck, rubbing the wide bright-red collar in his hands.

"No hunter will shoot her while she is wearing this thing. I hope not, anyway," he said distantly. The collar was Ken's idea. His plan was to have one last fish with Peaches and then put the collar on her neck to hopefully protect her from the upcoming hunting season. "Maybe I should put the collar on her first. You know, just in case she runs off or something," he said getting out of the truck.

Mark and I put on our waders and fishing vests as Ken called out for Peaches. The little deer did not come. Ken was obviously worried.

"She'll come around buddy," Mark said, stringing line through his rod. "We'll start fishing, and the next thing you know she will be ruining your best holes."

Ken put on his gear and we began working downstream. Ken would call out occasionally, searching the brush for his friend. She never came.

We fished that evening in silence. We never discussed it, but inside we all wondered where our little deer was. At the end of the night we stood by the old bridge watching as the last day of the fishing season slipped away. The sky turned blood-red and a late September chill floated down from the dark-green hills. Our gear was packed tightly in Mark's truck and we were ready to go, except for Ken. He walked down the road with the collar in hand calling out her name, hoping to protect her. Mark and I waited at his truck, leaning against the tailgate and hoping Peaches would come. We watched as Ken walked the dusty road a couple hundred feet away in silence. I was about to walk to him when he shouted, filling the still air with alarm. I will never forget the tone of his voice.

"Over here!" he yelled. "I hear something."

Mark and I ran down the road, following Ken who was crashing through the brush near the fence. He stood quietly as we approached.

It was the awful sound of wire being stretched and pulled against the posts that I remember most. A haunting sound of capture and pain. Peaches lay twisted in the wire mesh, the strands of barbed wire cutting deeply into her belly and neck. She lay bloody in the dead grass of autumn, her abdomen open and organs exposed. Small puffs of breath came from her nose and hung like whispers of pain in the heavy air. Peaches looked up helplessly at Ken.

"Get my medical kit!" Ken screamed at me, his eyes streaming with tears as he pulled frantically at the wire. "And your toolbox," he shouted to Mark, who was already several feet down the road. I ran behind, reaching the truck as Mark was pulling out the toolbox and medical kit. He did not see me reach into my pack and slide the large handgun into my belt.

When we came back to Ken he was bloody to the elbows. His hands were cut from the barbed wire and his shirt was torn from the deer's flailing hooves. Mark began cutting her free with a heavy set of wire cutters, his hands shaking as each strand broke free with a loud snap. I stood by them both, pulling freshly cut wire out of the way yet knowing that the situation was hopeless.

"Pull her over here!" Ken gasped, his voice cracking with emotion and physical exertion. He dug in his kit, pulling out two bottles of saline and a roll of gauze.

"Her hind legs are broken," Mark said, looking at me, then to Ken.

Ken did not respond. He washed away the blood from her belly, revealing the foot long gash and torn intestines.

"She's not going to survive, Ken," I said slowly. "Even without the broken legs, she's torn up too bad in her abdomen. She's been like this for hours, even a day or more. You know infection must be roaring in her."

Ken knew I was right. He stroked her neck and whispered to her softly. Peaches was calm now. Her labored breathing had slowed to nearly nothing as she looked up helplessly at Ken. I pulled the pistol from my belt and let it hang along my side. "Do you want me to do this?" I asked.

Ken looked to me than back at Peaches. "I'll meet you back at the truck," he said, reaching out and taking the gun.

Mark and I walked slowly down the dusty road toward the old bridge. It was dark now, with only the moonlight casting a glow on the rolling hills and tumbling stream. A whippoorwill called out in a lonely voice. We leaned against Mark's truck, listening to the crickets and the night sounds moving across the meadow. In the distance, the hills were silhouetted against the night sky, appearing lonely but peaceful. I looked into the blackness where Peaches used to lay beneath the alders, seeing her dainty body and deep brown eyes. I remembered how she looked so content in the rich green ferns—when the shot rang out so clearly on that quiet night.

KING OF THE DIAMOND

"**A**LAN, WE REALLY NEED TO TALK ABOUT THE TITLE FOR THIS chapter." My editor's face held the same expression that my junior high English teacher, Miss Walker, used to have when she grilled me on prepositional phrases. "I like the story, but the title is too long. Couldn't you find one that would describe the chapter using *four words or less*?" I decided to tease her.

"But, 'How The Combination of Stale Pistachio Nuts, a Spilled Pepsi, Numb Legs, and Gullies Grave Cost Me the Largest Deer of My Life,' so accurately describes the story!" My editor set the manuscript on the desk and rubbed her eyes like a parent who is setting curfew for a fifteen-year-old. "I mean, don't you think that shortening the title will take away from the story's *artistic* merit?" I shot her my best cocker spaniel puppy-pout for effect.

She grabbed a freshly sharpened yellow pencil and tapped the eraser on the desk, choosing her words carefully. "Alan," she said slowly. "Leo Tolstoy thought *War and Peace* was sufficient for his epic novel. I think something simple would work for one chapter in *Standing Ground*."

"Yeah, but did Leo hunt deer?"

She nearly impaled me with the pencil that, luckily, sailed past my shoulder.

"When you can *write* like Tolstoy, I will consider a longer title. Until then, CHANGE IT!"

"Okay, okay, I'll come up with something. By the way, are you drinking too much caffeine? You look a little tense."

She gave me the same look my mother used when I came home after curfew. "See what you can do," she said sternly.

I guess she *was* right. The title was far too long. The problem was that a story such as this requires an unusual beginning.

My grandfather owns eighty acres of farmland that is separated into two forty-acre parcels by an old gravel road. The north forty, as we call it, is leased to a local farmer for crops and is bordered by a stand of oaks. The south forty is mostly open field, leased to the same farmer, except for a small rectangle near the road. That is where my grandfather created his special place.

Grandpa built a large gazebo that he filled with used furniture and more than well used picnic tables. The walls hold various plaques that are sold by other grandfathers at county fairs and craft shows. Stuff like; *Grandpa's Place, Rules for the Outhouse, Beware of the Grandchildren,* that kind of thing.

Next to the gazebo is an ancient yellow travel trailer that year by year settles deeper on a bunch of cement blocks. Grandpa calls it the guesthouse, even though no one has used it for twenty years, except for shade. Beyond the trailer is a softball field with odd-shaped pieces of plywood for bases. An old wooden bench sits crookedly behind home plate next to the *Privy Up Yonder* sign. A little further yet is the goof ball course. Always looking for alternative forms of entertainment, Grandpa designed and built this nine-hole spoof of golf. Large blue Maxwell House coffee cans are buried in the ground for the holes. Homemade putters that look like hockey sticks on steroids serve as the tools for hitting tennis balls into the depths of the rusting cans.

Looming over all of this is a giant weeping willow that shades the area and a good portion of the pond Grandpa stocked with bluegills and bass. He called them his little pets, and they were, for the most part. Brightly colored bluegills, sunfish, and pumpkinseeds drifted though the warm water like tiny jewels, while good-sized bass hung deeper, using the shadows as cover and only coming out to take one of the pan fish. Grandpa used to feed them, daily in fact, with bread-crumbs and worms he dug under the willow. So used to his feeding, the smaller fish would follow him as he walked around the green edges of the pond. The bass would stay out of sight, except for one.

Grandpa named him Gully, for reasons I never quite understood. The adventurous bass would charge out among the small fish and compete for the food. After only one season, Grandpa could kneel down on the soft green bank and feed the bass while it was only a few feet away. The following spring Gully was back, smacking bread and worms only inches from his hands. By that fall, the fish took live worms from my grandfather's fingers. I'm not kidding. There is pho-tographic evidence.

For the next eight years, Grandpa fed his pet bass to proportions unknown outside of a Florida Bass Masters tournament. As the ice left the pond on Gully's eleventh year, Grandpa went to the pond to find him floating in the shallow end. We had a funeral, of course, and it was complete with a fairly large casket, larger headstone, and an even larger crowd of family and friends. Grandpa read a well-writ-ten eulogy and left a handful of wiggling worms at the base of the headstone. Gully's grave sits between the *Privy Up Yonder* sign and the tee off point for goof ball.

Aside from Grandpa's place being used for family gatherings, it was crawling with deer. Pet deer, really; the deer hung out in the nearby pine forest and fed in the corn and alfalfa fields all summer and fall. Deer that used to wander in the fields while four generations of Murray's tossed breadcrumbs into the pond and played goof ball. Mostly there were does and fawns, but occasionally there would be a small buck, at least until hunting season.

When November 15th came, the preferred national holiday of central Michigan, and when the local schools closed and all able-bodied men dressed in day-glow orange and took to the wilds of farm fields and hunting shacks, few bucks were to be seen. I, too, felt the call of the wild, but never hunted Grandpa's land. This was mainly because I knew most of the deer on a personal level, having watched them frolic in the fields all summer. No, my hunting trips were in the great north woods, where I would spend days searching the deep forests for buck rubs and scrapes and scouring the brush for signs of the *big one*. I hunted the king of the woods. The monster buck. The one that never came.

This year was different. With my work as liaison officer in the schools and as an author promoting my first book, I had little time for extended hunting trips, or even short jaunts in the woods. But I like to eat venison. A lot in fact, so when the fabled day approached, I decided I could go to Grandpa's and perhaps shoot a small buck or even a fat doe to have some sweet meat in the freezer.

Grandpa was pleased to have me come down for opening morning. He was not able to hunt this year, but was up early to see that I had a breakfast big enough to fuel a battleship. He told of several small bucks working the place and suggested several areas to watch.

I left Grandpa's with a full belly and parked near the gazebo. The eastern sky was beginning to show signs of light as I sat under a crooked pine tree near hole seven of the goof ball course. It wasn't really hunting, at least not the kind of hunting I was used to. No more than thirty feet from my truck and less than ten feet from Gully's headstone and the *Privy Up Yonder* sign, I felt more like I was waiting in a park than stalking white-tailed deer. I looked across the softball diamond to the cornfield beyond and studied the ridge. I knew that any deer in the field would come over that ridge when the first shots rang out at daybreak. They would want the cover of the pine forest behind me. So I got comfortable. It was nearly fifty degrees, with almost no wind. I opened a bottle of Pepsi and took out my bag of pistachio nuts that had been sitting in my truck for several weeks. As dawn approached and the sky lightened and the first shots came, I was comfortable under my pine tree. The only other sound that morning was the constant crack of the stale nuts as I pried them open with my fingers, and the fizz as I washed them down with Pepsi. By full daylight, the nuts were half gone and their shells covered the stock of my rifle that lay across my lap.

I saw the deer just as I was struggling with a rather tough nut. With a final thrust of my thumb, I pulled apart the shell, only to cut my thumb deeply with the hull. While trying to stop the bleeding, I saw movement from the corner of my eye. I did not see the whole deer, just his antlers coming over the ridge. Now, I've had buck fever before, many times in fact, but this was different, mainly because I was not expecting to see any deer that large and especially because I was watching the huge set of antlers across my grandpa's softball field. With the deer's body hidden beyond the ridge, only his tall rack of antlers showed above, tall and filled with ten points, at least. I watched the sun glisten off the polished bone and reflect back to me as he moved to my right. In moments he would be clear of the ridge and in a perfect position for a shot. I tried to move to my knees, but suddenly realized that sitting under the pine tree had caused both of my legs to fall asleep. They would not respond. Leaning over, I tried to crawl away from the tree and spilled my Pepsi, which foamed and bubbled under my hip. Looking up, I saw the great head of the deer as he moved cautiously across the field, approaching second base. From a prone position, I attempted to aim as he came into full view near the shortstop area. I had a clear shot, so I reached up to take off the rifle's safety, but winced when the deep cut in my thumb raked across the lever. Pain shot up my arm, but I pushed anyway. The blood prevented any traction on the metal. I tried several times but could not push the safety off. I reached around and pushed it forward with my left thumb, just as he rounded third and was coming for home. Before I could find his chest in the cross hairs, my shot was blocked by Gully's headstone. At this point my legs began to get some feeling. It felt like they were full of painful tickles. I pulled myself forward on the grass and tried to get beyond the headstone. In the process I smashed the bag of pistachio nuts, making a loud crunch. The deer's head shot toward me as he stopped. I froze as he looked at me. Moments passed before his tail went up. I could tell he was about to bolt. I brought up the rifle for a shot just as he jumped past home plate and back over the ridge. "Safe!" I yelled after him.

OWL PEOPLE

THE PARKING AREA WAS DESERTED. ACTUALLY IT WASN'T MUCH OF a parking area, just a clearing in the spruce forest where the National Park Service dumped several hundred yards of road gravel to make a flat spot in an otherwise lumpy woods. A light rain, the kind common in Southeast Alaska in spring, summer, and fall, spattered my patrol unit's windshield and peppered the many puddles in the brown gravel. I sat for several minutes behind the wheel trying to decide if I wanted to see the cemetery today or wait for better weather. Looking toward the dark woods, I saw the historical plaque and yellow arrow pointing down a trail covered in wood chips. It was almost dark and the drizzle, along with the low clouds, would make night approach faster on this early spring day. The lack of police complaints and the boredom created by too much time spent alone made me decide to have a look at the last unexplored landmark in my patrol area.

With the unit's engine off I felt the quietness flow around me as I stood in the wet gravel and smelled the rich scent of spruce and rotting plant life on the forest floor. I turned up the collar of my police jacket and stepped carefully to avoid the deeper puddles. Walking into the darkness of the woods, I approached the marker, taking time to read the account through the wet glass. An owl called from deep

in the forest, its hoot sounding like a warning. I thought about return-
ing to the unit and back to town, but read through the water-covered
glass instead.

It was the spring of 1898, April 3rd to be exact. Palm Sunday. A
group of prospectors and their families made a camp at the base of
this mountain. They were only a half-mile or so from Dyea and came
here, it is assumed, to escape the crowds of the gold-rush boomtown.
In 1898 Dyea was a city of twenty thousand, with each person either
waiting to cross into Canada's Yukon Territory for the gold fields or
working in the city, taking money from the hopefuls. Each day more
ships would travel the Inside Passage and unload more prospectors,
each of whom assumed they would find wealth in the Klondike. After
purchasing supplies and often buying poor advice from merchants in
Dyea, the people would begin the sixteen-mile journey over the
Chilkoot Pass and along the chain of lakes that would connect them
to the gold fields. The fifty or so people decided to make camp at the
mountain's base and wait for better weather to begin their journey.
They never left.

Sometime during the early morning hours of April 3rd, an
avalanche roared down the mountainside and slammed into the
valley, burying several acres of forest and all trace of the camp. In
seconds nothing was left but rock-hard snow and the trees brought
down the mountain by the avalanche. So total was the destruction
and so deep was the debris, it was weeks before anyone in Dyea
knew how many were killed. The melting snow of the Alaskan spring
slowly left the mountain's base and displayed what once was a
happy and hopeful community.

Because of the lack of identification that could be found and the
condition of the bodies, the people of Dyea simply buried the dead

where they lay. Some names were found among papers, but most were put in unmarked graves. Simple markers of wood were erected among the trees. Although most of the markers deteriorated quickly, they were replaced every decade or so by the people of Skagway. Today the National Park Service maintains the gravesite known as the Slide Cemetery.

Fresh wood chips covered the trail leading away from the parking area. They were a sharp contrast to the rusty-brown spruce and pine needles littering the forest floor. The constant drizzle made the chips soft and quiet, so that my footsteps made almost no sound. Raindrops fell from high branches, spatting on the larger limbs and then running down the tree trunks. Spanish moss covered in droplets hung from the low branches. The winding trail went only a hundred feet before I saw the first grave. What I expected was a conventional cemetery. What I found was disturbing.

The graves were scattered among the trees around me. I walked to the closest and looked at the rough pine slab. I bent down and felt the letters cut deeply into the wood. *Male, about age thirty*, it read. Below was *Died, April 3, 1898*. I brushed away some pine needles from the top and thought about the man who lay beneath my feet. He would have been expecting riches in the gold fields. He was on a quest. I looked up to another grave just beyond a large hemlock. Walking over, I saw this marker was a white cross. The paint was peeling but I could still read the inscription. *Baby, died April 3, 1898*. I leaned against the hemlock and felt the dampness of the bark. I looked around at the others. The markers stood in all directions, each with the same date. I felt like I was trespassing on holy ground, or perhaps a tormented place. An owl called again, closer this time.

Normally the silence of the woods is comforting to me. This was different. I began to have an uneasy feeling, a feeling that I was not alone. I walked among the graves and felt the heaviness of the air, the constant dripping from the trees, and the feeling that I was intruding.

The graves were everywhere. Tucked behind trees, scattered in clearings, and grouped in small pods. When I reached the back of the cemetery, I came to the base of the mountain. There were several graves there, but I could not read the inscriptions. I looked up at the mountain and imagined the killing snow crashing through the trees. Looking back at the graves, I could see how the entire area was covered.

Darkness was coming quickly, and now a heavy mist drifted through the damp trees mixing with the constant dripping of the rain. Suddenly I felt uneasy. I was just about to leave for my patrol unit when I heard the voices.

They weren't ghostly voices or cries of pain or fear like I might have expected. They were just voices. I could hear them distantly, like being in a far corner of a house and hearing people talking in another room. I shivered slightly and began to have the feeling of being watched. Not menacingly, just watched, like people were all around me, wondering what I was doing and at the same time glad that I was here. Somehow I felt a part of all this.

I walked quickly back to my patrol unit and returned to town. I never told anyone what I heard. It was eight years before I returned.

Mark looked at me with his sideways glance when I stopped the rental car in the parking area. We had been out for a drive after a book signing in Skagway and I was showing him some of the places I had written about in *Alaska Behind Blue Eyes*. We were on our way to the bridge over West Creek when I stopped.

"So, are you taking me parking or something?" he asked. Mark looked out the window at the forest. It was late in the evening, but because it was near the solstice, sunlight streaked through the trees making the woods seem vibrant. "Don't see a river," he said.

"There is something I want you to see. Actually, I want you to experience something. Don't ask any questions. Just look around and tell my what you feel," I said slowly. Mark was used to my strange requests and stepped out of the car and began walking toward the information plaque. "Wait!" I said, walking quickly to catch up with him. "Don't read that. Just follow me."

I sent Mark down the trail that was covered with another layer of fresh wood chips. I lagged behind, watching. He finally came to a grave and it startled him. What is this place?" he asked.

I said nothing and leaned against a spruce tree. Mark looked closely at the writing and seemed confused. "No name. Just a marker and a date," he said. He saw another and walked to it. "This is the same date. What is this place?" I wanted to explain but motioned with my hand for him to continue.

The sound startled me, bringing back emotions that I left here eight years before. The owl called again in the deepness of the forest. Shivers went up my spine. *They're still here*, I thought to myself. Mark walked through the cemetery and looked at each grave. He reached the base of the mountain and knelt beside a battered marker, pulling away dead needles and twigs. Turning his head toward me his face was serious.

"What happened here?" he asked.

"Avalanche," I answered.

"All were killed?"

"Yes."

Mark stood and put his hands in his pockets. He looked to the deep-green canopy above him and took a heavy breath of the rich air. "You know, it's almost weird. I can feel them around me. Not bad, really, it's just that somehow I can feel a presence. Funny, I never felt this way in any other cemetery." My friend walked to my side and looked at me. "You knew what I would feel, didn't you?"

"Yes."

The owl called again, its hoot sharp and close. Mark looked in the direction and started walking toward the car. "The owl plays a part in all this, right?"

"Yes. I will tell you about it some time," I said, following behind.

THE DIFFICULT BREED

"HI. MY NAME IS ALAN AND I HAVE OWNED A LABRADOR Retriever for eight years."

The quiet crowd that is sitting on old folding chairs in the dusty basement of the pet supply store reply in unison. "Hi Alan," they say in a supportive monotone.

"The other day he ate two of our kitchen chairs. He's getting better, though. Last year he ate the table."

"That's okay, Alan," they say together. "He'll grow out of it someday."

I step away from the podium and walk to the refreshment table on the way back to my seat. I pour some weak coffee in a Styrofoam cup and sit near the back of the room. A rather frazzled-looking woman steps to the podium as I sip from the cup.

"Hi. My name is Monica. I have owned a Labrador Retriever for seven months," she says in a shaky voice that we veteran retriever owners remember well.

The room fills with the squeak of metal chairs being pushed rapidly back as we all stand and clap. Shouts of, "You'll make it through the first year, Monica!" and "Don't give up, it will get better!" fill the crowded room.

Monica grins politely and pulls a piece of leather from her purse. She holds it before the crowd. "This is all that I have left of my sofa," she says. The people nod and smile collectively, remembering their first digested piece of furniture. Monica sits in the front row and waits for the next person to address the group.

It's not easy owning a Labrador Retriever. Luckily for me I learned that there was a local chapter of L.R.O.S.S (Labrador Retriever Owners Support System) in town. The group meets weekly in the basement of a pet food and supply store amid stacks of dog food bags and wire travel cages. It's a good organization. Friendly, caring people meet four times each month to lend support during the most difficult years of Labrador Retriever ownership, which are, by the way, the first fifteen. After that, the animals are too old to destroy more than a small table lamp. For those readers not familiar with the joys of Labrador ownership, I offer, as a service to all, some information on the breed. I'll begin with a little history.

Long, long ago in a land far away from Clare, Michigan, there was a group of evil men who, among other things, decided to overthrow the Provence of Labrador. They also happened to be expert dog breeders. Their plan was simple; develop a species of evil dog the country-folk would take into their homes as pups. As the puppies rapidly became full-grown dogs, the citizens would find their property slowly destroyed and the breeders could *retrieve* the country they wished to rule. It was a simple plan, and creative, but it failed because the evil ones neglected to consider one important aspect of the breed. That is, their new breed, known as *Labrador Retriever*, had none of their evil ways. The dogs loved their owners even though they gnawed at the foundations of their homes.

The original Labrador Retriever was a cross between a Hereford bull (for strength and stubbornness), a beaver (for gnawing ability), a baby duck (for cuteness when young), and an alligator (for a tail that can knock over small trees). The wonder of Labradors is that as pups they are about the most attractive thing in the world. Few people can resist picking up such a cute bundle of fur and feet. This, you see, is how they work their way into people's lives.

Labrador Retrievers come in three colors. There is aggravation-yellow, why-did-we-ever-get-this stupid-dog black, and a combination of the two which is, let's-give-this-dog-to-my-mother-in-law chocolate.

My family's Labrador came into our home as a five-pound bundle of energy, covered in a shimmering coat of rich chocolate hair. With bright yellow eyes and a quizzical grin, he soon won the hearts of our household. I named him Taku (ta-coo) after a beautiful glacier in Alaska. For the first several weeks, he behaved like any good puppy. He rarely messed in the house. He padded around looking for attention and was always alert for intruders. I would look at him sleeping soundly next to my favorite chair and envision him next to me in the duck blind, watching the skies for south-bound flocks. He was, I was sure, going to be the perfect dog.

By the time he was four months old and weighed about forty pounds, I was ready to kill him and not feel the least bit guilty. Death-by-owner is, by the way, the second leading cause of a Labrador's demise. The first is death-by-eating-something-impossible-to-digest.

At four months of age, Taku developed the disease that inflicts all Labrador pups. It is called *Chewonstuff Syndrome*. It began innocently enough. Shredded laces from dress shoes were found on the bedroom floor, missing corners of books from the shelf littered most rooms, and tattered trash bags turned into smelly confetti littered the kitchen and garage. Not being familiar with the disease, I smiled and cleaned up after the pup, knowing that this must be a passing phase.

After all, he would look up from the shoe with that classic I'm-sorry head-tilt expression and melt my heart. *A little gentle scolding was all he needed,* I thought. I raised a Golden Retriever from a young pup and could correct his occasional mistakes with a stern look. *Taku would be no different,* I thought. I was wrong.

Taku graduated from chewing up simple things to simply chewing everything. Although we watched him constantly, more and more of our home was being passed through the digestive tract of a forty-pound dog with irresistible facial expressions. Thinking he needed more exercise, we allowed him to romp endlessly in the backyard where he, among other things, discovered a passion for retrieving dead and dying rodents. Taku also took advantage of his outdoor adventures to pursue the natural enemy of the Labrador, the common ground mole.

In his never-ending quest to rid the world of the burrowing rodents, Taku would use his uncanny sense of smell to zero-in on a gray furry target, then use his giant paws to dig a crater large enough to hide a battle tank. Normally the mole would be acres away by the time he reached assault depth, but he remained undaunted. There were times when I would look out the window to find only the tail of my faithful friend wagging out of a hole large enough to fill with water and stock with fish. When confronted with this deed, Taku would look up from his digging with an expression best described as "Don't worry boss. I'll get him."

By the time he was eight months old, Taku had retained all of his chewing attributes and added another destructive habit. Weighing eighty pounds and in possession of a body like a plow horse with the drive of an army jeep stuck at full throttle, Taku took up the hobby of jumping on people. Because I still outweighed him by over a hundred fifty pounds, having his giant front feet strike my chest only caused me to stagger a bit. The rest of the family would usually be knocked to the floor. I attempted to stop this behavior by taking advice from other dog owners who, unfortunately, never owned a Labrador. They said to take his front paws firmly in my hands and squeeze. Dogs, they said with confidence, hate that. Right. Taku viewed this technique not as a punishment, but more as an offer to dance. Next, my non-Labrador owning friends suggested the quick-step-on-the-rear-feet-while-holding-the-front-paws method. This resulted in Taku doing his rendition of a fox trot while grinning up at me. Stronger methods would be needed, but I was determined not to break his spirit. However, after two weeks of chest jumping, I found that nothing short of a hand grenade in his mouth would break anything, including his spirit.

What cured Taku's jumping problem was a combination of anger and even more anger. One day I walked in the house after a long day of police work only to have my chocolate bundle of muscle jump on my chest with such force that his claws nearly penetrated my bullet-proof vest. Out of instinct and anger, I gave Taku a genuine police knee-strike to the chest that would have killed an average man. He flew back against the wall with a giant thud, crashing to the floor where he lay for several seconds trying to catch his breath. For a moment I thought I may have killed him and was trying to sort out whether I was happy or sad. Then he jumped to his feet and looked at me with an expression that said, "Excuse me. Is there a problem here?" He has never jumped on anyone since. This is also the point when I realized that a Labrador owner never really trains his pet, they just reach a mutual understanding.

Labradors have an extremely powerful tail that experts on the breed claim is used as a rudder while swimming. Although I hate to question the wisdom of those brave enough to proclaim themselves experts on an animal who views dead squirrels as one of life's simple pleasures, the only thing I have seen Taku use his tail for is knocking over end tables and bruising the shins of tall guests in my house.

After eight years of Labrador ownership, I find that Taku is no longer the destroyer of home furnishings he once was. Oh sure, he occasionally gnaws the rubber from the bumper of my truck or sometimes tears sections of vinyl siding from my house, but he does these things at a much slower pace than when he was a puppy.

And, he has become my faithful duck hunting companion. I enjoy watching him as he sits by my side in the duck blind, as the north wind blows strongly over the marsh and cattails bend back and forth. Overhead I can hear the faint whistling of Mallard wings. I look down. I watch as Taku enjoys the day, resting contentedly on the bottom of the boat as he absently removes small slivers from my gun stock.

SEEING LOVE

I'M NOT EXACTLY SURE HOW I WAS TALKED INTO TAKING THE KIDS TO a movie. It probably had something to do with the or else looks from my friends who said, without question, that the world would cease to exist if they failed to play golf at a distant course. Always one to protect the planet and support the golfing industry (it keeps people off *my* trout streams), I volunteered to help, using my best *you-owe-me-one* grin. This was somewhat of a veiled protest because, to be honest, I enjoyed spending time with their children. I just wanted the favor to seem like a significant sacrifice so that my buddies would feel a tinge of guilt on the putting greens.

A few hours later I found myself standing in a long line outside our local theater supervising several squirming cracker-crunchers. The movie we were waiting to see was Walt Disney's *Bambi*.

Of course, we had to sit in the front row, which allowed for the maximum distance to be traveled when buying the necessary popcorn, Junior Mints, and other assorted calorie-laden items for the kids. After I had made several sugar runs, long before the animated epic started, I began to secretly wish that Bambi would hurry up and become an orphan.

It had been so long since I had seen a movie that was not meant for people who regularly shave, that I had forgotten the wonders of the childhood theater-going experience. When I was young my parents would allow me to see any movie as long as it was rated G. Being brought up in Clare, a city with only one theater that only opened on the weekends, the large black letters appearing on the marquee were an open invitation to every prepubescent to, as we put it, "go to the show." No matter what the film was, if it was rated G, it meant go. Looking around the theater on this night, I was pleased to see that little had changed since my youth.

The older children, those who had reached the age to attend alone, were grouped in lightly structured cliques that spent the majority of their time moving from one location to another. In a way it was like a game of preteen chess where middle-school students sacrificed optimum viewing locations for the closeness of the opposite sex. To a middle-school student, the seating strategy was far more important than the feature.

The rich smell of popcorn filled the small theater with a heavy, high-fat fragrance. This aroma competed with the equally strong odor of spilled soft drinks, mint chewing gum, and dad's cologne.

I looked around to find that the only thing that had changed since I was eleven was the music. When I started going to the movies to meet my friends, the theater owner played a large variety of music before each show, although each song was by the Carpenters. For what seemed like years, I struggled with the anxiousness of pre-movie chess to the mellow voice of Karen Carpenter. To this day, hearing one of her old songs takes me immediately back to the Ideal Theater in Clare, and the wonder of popcorn and snapping gum.

I was quietly humming "We've Only Just Begun," when a man and a little girl approached our section of seats. They sat right behind us. I may not have noticed them at first, had I not been turned around to retrieve a dropped candy box. The little girl had one of those big grins that said she was glad to be with dad. Her father held her hand tightly as they maneuvered down the crowded aisle and settled down with a satisfied sigh. The girl was probably eight years old, although it was difficult to tell because she wore dark sunglasses that made her pretty face seem very small. I nodded to her father with that sympathetic look men give each other when they wish they were somewhere else but glad to be where they are—all at the same time.

Then, something unusual happened. The girl's father began to describe the theater to her in exact detail. He started with the paint color of the walls, the height of the ceiling, and the size and shape of the blue luminous clock near the screen. He continued with the exit sign, and the color of the seats, and the pattern of the carpet. He also told her how many people were in the theater and the ratio of children to adults. When others walked by, he said what they were wearing and how many were in their party. It finally occurred to me that his daughter was blind.

I was immediately saddened. *How could a blind girl possibly enjoy this experience, other than to be next to her dad?* Once the movie started, however, I began to understand the beauty of imagination and the deepness of a father's love.

In a quiet voice, nearly a whisper, he became her eyes. He described the on-screen characters in such detail that they became alive for his daughter. I soon closed my eyes and listened to his voice. I could clearly see the action as it unfolded. The combination of the movie's music and dialogue, with the man's descriptions, produced a richness that I had never before experienced. I saw every color and detail of Bambi and his forest friends as they romped through their adventure. His patient cadence of speech added a new dimension to a film that I had probably watched twenty times.

About halfway through the movie I reached over to Taylor, who was busy putting a Junior Mint up her nose. "Listen to the man behind us, Taylor. Just close your eyes and listen," I said softly.

Taylor shut her eyes tightly, wrinkling her pretty face. She paused, in intense determination for about thirty seconds, then looked up at me with wide eyes. "I can see it," she whispered. "I can see it all. This is neat!"

Taylor again shut her eyes and did her best to eat the mints without too much spillage. I could see her concentrate deeply as the man continued his narrative in a gentle voice. After several minutes she opened her eyes and spoke to Jessica, who was trying to find the remaining gummy bears that had tried to make an escape in her lap.

"Close your eyes and listen, Jessica," Taylor said in a very cute and yet serious tone. "Listen to the man behind us." Then, as an afterthought, she added, "Pass it on."

Jessica closed her eyes and within moments was grinning. She told Katlyn, who responded quickly and then told Kayla, who took a little longer than the others because of her current popcorn fight with Mitchell. However, before long, each of my charges had their eyes closed and were watching a great film being made more wonderful by the power of their mind's eye.

The two younger children were nearly asleep as I buckled their seatbelts. The warm August night was humid and still, and a full moon was just beginning to rise over the trees. It took several minutes to corral the rest of the kids to the confines of the van, but soon we were headed toward their homes. Mitchell and Jessica were quietly babbling on about something that was only important to them as I left the downtown lights of Clare. Taylor sat in the passenger seat, looking out her window with a deep-in-thought expression only possible in a seven-year-old. I could see that she was about to speak.

"Al," she said quietly, as if she did not want to disturb the others. "Do you think her dad tells her about everything?" Taylor continued looking out her window with studied concentration. "I mean, does he tell her about trees and puppies and fish and stuff like that?"

"I'm sure he does, Taylor. You see, she can use her mind to see the things her eyes cannot. Just like you did in the theater."

Taylor ran her small hand over the tan nylon of her seatbelt and lowered her head, closing her eyes tightly. "I'm sorry that she is blind, but I'm happy because she has a father who will tell her about things. Is that how he shows her that he loves her?"

I reached over and ran my hand over Taylor's long braided hair, giving it a playful tug. "Yes, Taylor," I said softly. "That is how she sees his love for her."

SOMETHING LARGE

MARK LOOKED DISTANTLY ACROSS THE MARSH WITH A HOPEFUL gaze, as if ducks could be willed to appear by thought alone. My eyes followed his to the far shore and the line of trees that aggressively announced the seasonal change. Sugar maples with leaves so bright red they looked like neon flashes shone against the brilliant gold of poplars and the dark-green from the pine and balsams. Across from us the cattails waved in unison, gently saluting the faint northerly breeze. Gentle wisps of wind pushed the flooding's still water from slate-gray to brightened patterns that became mosaic under the slight pressure. The sky was bright blue with no sign of a front that would drive down birds from the north. I looked down at the shotgun resting on my lap and carefully brushed away a few stray tufts of cattail fluff, enjoying the pleasant temperature and waiting out the last hour of shooting time.

"Bluebird day," Mark said. "Be lucky if we see any flocks tonight."

I did not answer. He was right, of course. Mark always was when it came to ducks or any other hunting pursuit. Still, I was hopeful. Well, perhaps not hopeful, but at least randomly wishful. This internal optimism is necessary with duck hunters who, among other things, require some sort of confidence to spend countless hours in a tiny boat in a large wetland waiting for something that may or may not appear. Still, I knew his observation was correct. If not a good day for hunting, it was at least a good day to think.

Days like this are for deep thoughts. At times like this I often think of the past, especially the part of the past that men turn to with time to daydream. I thought of my shyness as a high school senior. I wondered why I always become overly emotional whenever a friend has a baby. I wonder if I will ever be a father. While I am here, I wonder what kind of father I would be.

"You're thinking deep thoughts again," Mark stated simply. He took off his hat and scratched his graying hair, taking time to study the faded camouflage pattern. "I can always tell. You get that 'poor me' look and a droopy face."

"It's nothing."

"Right," Mark replied. He pulled the hat snugly over his head and looked back across the water. "Whatever you say."

Only a faint orange glow was left of the sun as it sank behind the trees. The breeze was gone now, leaving a perfect stillness over the water. Huge bands of yellow and red stretched over the marsh like a giant circus tent slowly encompassing the earth beneath. The cattails were still, standing tall and straight, a dark mass pressing against the water. I always liked this time of day. Not quite day and not quite night. It is a time of transformation. The witching hour.

"That's it," Mark said, looking at his watch. He pulled down the camouflage netting from the front of the boat and cased his gun. "You still with me?" he asked.

I again did not answer. Taking one of the oars, I pushed the pram out of the reeds and into our set of decoys. The sky grew darker and the colors deepened before becoming a mixed array of shades, like a child that over-blends Play-Doh and stops just before it becomes an ugly brown. We picked up the dozen blocks and piled them between the boat seats.

Each oar stroke cut the water deeply, creating a depression that quickly filled in and became whole in the watery stillness. I liked to watch the oars as I rowed, seeing the steady movement of dark water and hearing the faint whispers from the oar locks. It was only a couple hundred yards to the launch. Actually, it was just an opening in the forest where the marsh willows were thin and the water was deep. Mark guided me in silence, using only a few gestures with his hands to direct us to the opening.

The bow of the pram nudged the muddy shore with a satisfying hiss, followed by a sudden stop. Mark crawled slowly from the boat and pulled the little craft a few more feet out of the water. He paused for a moment and looked out across the water. I stepped over the decoys and netting to help him with the remaining distance, but stopped by his side to also look over the marsh.

Only the soft glow of sunset remained behind the tree line, outlining the forest and creating a black uneven line. The brilliant colors of only a half-hour before had faded and left only a few soft red splashes and some faint streaks of yellow. The sky was quickly turning deep gunpowder gray. A few stars appeared, twinkling and looking like they were testing the heavenly grounds for others to follow.

It was peaceful to be here and watch as nature went to sleep. The breeze had disappeared, leaving only calmness in the remaining moments of light. I thought of my past and future and wondered what Mark was thinking. *Probably about his family,* I guessed. We stood together, enjoying the total lack of sound and the comfort of an old friend who knew when silence was enough.

"Can you ever remember a night this still?" Mark asked. He put his hands into his coat pocket and sighed deeply. "Sometimes the quiet is scary, isn't it?"

I shrugged my shoulders and kicked at a small tuft of grass. "It's the unknown that is scary."

It came from across the marsh, beyond the tree line and deep within the swamp. Four deep grunts, which sounded like anger being pushed through the body of something dangerous, flowed across the still water and bathed us in astonishment. Each grunt was raspy and hollow and filled with what seemed to be a pent-up rage. The next sound began as a low howl, then rose sharply to a siren-like wail. At the end of this sound was a hideous scream that echoed up and down the marsh with an intensity I had never experienced. It left the silence in a weakened state.

The marsh was now once again still, but different somehow. The sound reverberated in my ears.

"What . . . was that?" Mark asked, without looking away from the far side of the marsh.

Before I could answer, it happened again. The raw power of the beginning grunts sent chills down my spine until the siren cry raced across the water and found me standing, dumbstruck. My hair was standing on end. Mark looked ready to faint.

"I'll back up the truck," I said, reaching for my keys and walking away. Mark pulled the boat to the truck on his own, and within minutes we were loaded. We started down the two- track trail in silence, each wanting to know what it was, but both too scared to know.

"Bear?" I asked, knowing the answer.

"No."

"That was no coyote or owl or lynx," I stated.

"I know," Mark replied. "What about a wolf? You ever hear wolves sound like that in Alaska?"

"No, not even close."

"Then what in the hell was it?" Mark asked. He looked out the window at the passing trees illuminated by the headlights. "I mean, between the two of us we have heard about all the sounds in the northern woods except, of course, that."

"Whatever it is, it's large. Something across the marsh has a large chest and, apparently, much to say," I said quietly. Mark was silent for several minutes, as we continued through the woods. We were nearly to the main road when he spoke.

"Do you want to continue guessing?" he asked.

"No."

"Are we going to tell our other friends about tonight?"

"No," I answered.

Somewhere in Michigan, in a giant swamp beyond a beautiful marsh, is something large. It or they remain silent much of the time unless it or they choose to be heard. I remember the incident like a distant memory that still haunts me. Something scary and thought provoking, but all the same, enchanting. I am glad, regardless of the outcome, that things like this remain.

CLOSET BAIT FISHERMAN

OPENING DAY OF TROUT SEASON IN MICHIGAN IS ALWAYS THE last Saturday in April. After several long months of winter, most of which take place in February, this first day of the season is often viewed more like a holiday than a Saturday spent with a fishing pole. When I was in seventh grade, my new friend Bud asked me to fish with him on this hallowed date. Bud had the fortune of living next to the Tobacco River, which is home to many species of fish, including trout.

We planned our first-day adventure for weeks, going over each detail of our river assault to the point of obsession. Long before the advent of graphite rods and sophisticated equipment, our gear was culled from whatever we could borrow, generally without their knowledge, from our dads. This planning resembled more of a battle plan than a day of pleasant fishing. Stout fiberglass rods that were stiff and connected to closed-faced reels the size of melons were dusted off and readied. Each rod was strung with thick monofilament line that could pull a Buick from a muddy ditch. Thick wire hooks were attached with a series of half-hitch knots and heavy sinkers were added about a foot above. Our bait was the common nightcrawler. Assembling our stock of "crawlers" was an adventure in itself.

To procure a batch of slimy dirt eaters required a dark night, heavy rain, flashlights, and the reflexes of barn cats on speed. Our favorite hunting ground was my front yard that, during a heavy night rain, turned from a flat expanse of green to a hunting ground for large worms. The warm spring rain saturated the ground, forcing the crawlers to the surface where they didn't exactly frolic, but at least hung out for awhile. The procedure was simple: walk slowly across the lawn until your flashlight beam fell on one, then try to catch it before the worm could retreat back into the soggy earth. Although a simple technique, the actual act was somewhat more difficult. For an organism with a brain the size of a dust speck, the night crawlers were surprisingly quick. Only because of the huge number of worms were we successful. In an hour or so we had enough for fishing and came in from the rain looking like wet slime-covered dogs.

Bud's river contained trout, suckers, chubs, sunfish, rock bass and a host of little large-scaled fish that had an ability to remove crawlers from hooks with a precision only found in vascular surgeons. The river flowed swiftly behind his house then made a bend, creating a large and deep pool. In the hazy light of dawn, still buzzing from a night spent drinking highly caffeinated soft drinks and talking endlessly about the girls in our class, with the vast majority of comments centered around their rapid and wonderful developments, we trudged to the river with high hopes and tired eyes.

We actually caught fish! Most of our catches were suckers and annoying little fish of unknown origin, but we were catching fish. It was these early days of streamside pleasure that formed the basis for my now legendary fishing enthusiasm.

Somewhere between the time of my first love and finding out the joys of owning a vehicle, I began to drift in my fishing methods. From bait I slid into lures, and finally, after reading most of Hemingway's works, particularly his *Big Two Hearted River*, I became a fly fisherman.

In Alaska I used the long rod to catch, and mostly release, a great variety of fish. The grayling became my favorite, by far because of their aggressive strikes and the clear and beautiful rivers and streams in which they lived. In the high country lakes, I made long casts to small, but spirited brook trout and, on one special lake, large rainbows.

So I became a fly fishing snob. I guess there are worse things to admit, like my collection of Barry Manilow albums, or that my favorite part of a high school football game is to watch the opposing squads of cheerleaders greet each other like cats with claws extended. After all, I had evolved to a higher plane.

In time I acquired an extensive collection of fly rods, much to the dismay of my wife, that together represented more money than I spent on my first two cars. I had rods for large fish, small fish, fish in small streams, fish in large rivers and lakes, and two rods only to be used on special occasions. My favorite rod, an Orvis top-of-the-line, cost over five hundred dollars, not including the fine reel and fly line. All of this equipment was purchased to tempt frolicking speckled trout that weighed, on average, about the same as a large piece of beef jerky. Just assembling, donning, and carrying my equipment represented nearly two thousand dollars, if you include my bulging fishing vest. Then, there was the expensive clothing, which included a genuine Australian felt hat.

Being an in-the-flesh fly fishing semi-expert was not lost on my friends and people with whom I had contact. I would often be invited to a fishing excursion where the other participants would be using lures or bait with me arriving with only a fly rod. They would teasingly offer a can of worms, then laugh as I would shrink away in mock horror. This, of course, presented several problems. The truth was, as much as I hate to admit it, that for years I have been a closet bait fisherman.

Never forgetting the pleasures of my youthful fishing adventures with Bud, I occasionally longed for the sweet smell of an early spring morning and the feel of a fat night crawler between my fingers. Now, living alongside the South Branch of the Tobacco River, a stream filled with a variety of fish that *occasionally* includes trout, I find that the first warm days of the year bring back memories of the simple pleasures of my youth.

This spring the pull of these wonderful times was so strong that I dug out my old spinning outfit and even found some small brass hooks and lead sinkers. The river behind my house is fairly isolated, and I felt that I could fish the *old way* without detection from my neighbors. The only problem was obtaining the necessary bait. I have found as I grow older that crawling around in a rain shower in the dark looking for slimy things is not exactly number one on my list of fun things to do, even with the pull of nostalgic fishing memories. This meant a trip to a bait store. The problem was, because I was known by virtually everyone in town for my fly-fishing passion, I would have to pick an out-of-the-way store and go in semi-disguise. My first attempt was a failure.

I wore a large baseball cap displaying the emblem of a power equipment company and some dark sunglasses. I tried not to make eye contact with the storeowner as I approached the counter. He greeted me with that friendly, *What can I do for you*, look and waited for my request.

"Ah, I was wondering if you had a couple dozen crawlers?"

"Say, aren't you Alan White? You're the one who wrote that Alaska book, right? Got it for Christmas. Say, you're a big fly fisherman!"

"I, ah . . . I'm buying them for a friend," I said, feeling like I was holding a fake fishing I.D. card.

"Oh, I see," the man said, turning and checking an ancient refrigerator behind the counter. "Sorry, Mr. White. I am plum out. Can you check back in a couple days?"

I was already out the door and into the safety of my truck.

There was only one alternative left. I would have to drive to Beaverton. Beaverton is a little town far away enough from Clare that not many people know me. I started driving, determined to pick up a couple dozen symbols of my childhood. I was about halfway there when I began to laugh. Beaverton was a very important town when I was a much younger man. My friends and I used to make regular trips over the many miles of bad roads to buy *things* that we just could not in a town where every storeowner knew us. What made me laugh was that on this trip, I was headed for a bait store—not a drugstore.

As was the norm in Beaverton, no one knew me, and I was able to buy several dozen night crawlers, although I got that same old nervous and somewhat guilty feeling as when I was young and the pharmacist handed me a package with a knowing smile.

Later that afternoon I stood deep in the river behind my house, feeling the cold water on my waders and the feel of slime between my fingers. Bud would have been proud.

TWENTY-NINE SOUTH

T HE SOUTH WING DOOR IS NARROW ENOUGH TO SNAG THE ambulance cot each time my partner and me enter the building, and every time it does I become a little more aggravated. This entry through the door is the third time today—and the tenth time this week that I parked the ambulance in the rear parking lot and had to fight to push the cot from the steamy summer air into the hot stale air inside the nursing home. My partner moves ahead and holds the door, while I push the long, sheet-covered cot onto the gray industrial carpet of the narrow hallway. The door slams behind him, leaving us in the dim depressing light created by the tan block walls and dusty fluorescent lights. We head down the hall toward the nurses' station to pick up the file on our next patient.

We are immediately assaulted by the smell. No matter how much the staff wipes, scrubs, and washes, the odor of stale urine permeates the air. Nothing smells quite like a nursing home.

The nursing supervisor looks up from her papers and gives us a distant smile. She reaches for a neat color-coded file folder and thrusts it toward us with practiced efficiency. "Twenty-nine South," she dryly says, looking back to her papers. For the third time today we start down the hall, moving the cot past wheelchair-bound patients and the quiet cries and murmurs coming from the dim rooms. Twenty-nine South is the same as the others. I look in the open door, past the empty first bed, to the occupied second bed and wish that I were doing anything else but this.

Officially they are called nursing home transports. It is a service provided by the ambulance company, with a charge of course, where highly trained and experienced paramedics pick up nursing home patients, drive them to the local hospital for tests, then deliver them back to their beds. Generally the tests are routine examinations, with an occasional check for medical concerns.

I would usually pick up an unresponsive or nearly comatose patient, stand around the hospital while he or she had a simple test, then drop the person off and wait for the next run. While working the day shift I performed so many of these calls that I longed for a real emergency so I could use some of my more advanced paramedic skills. With nursing home runs there was only the quick check of blood pressure, a check of the pulse, and a few notes scribbled on a billing chart. Most of the time I felt more like a delivery person than a medical professional. That was, of course, until today.

Although it was nearly ninety degrees in the room, the only occupant of Twenty-nine South was curled under a blanket and sheet. She was tiny (most nursing home patients are) and looked like a skin-covered skeleton in a tall hospital bed with too many covers. I moved the cot alongside her bed and grabbed the thick bed pad. My partner moved to the other side and together we slid her onto our cot. The old woman looked up at me through dull gray eyes, as if she had just woken up. "We're taking you to the hospital," I said in my professional but patronizing voice that always seemed to come out when I transported nursing home patients.

Number Twenty-nine South tried to say something, but she stopped when I moved the top sheet over her frail body and snapped the belts over her legs, hips, and chest. I took the head of the cot and pulled her quickly out the door and down the hall with my partner guiding the rear.

I saw her wince at the sunlight as we squeezed back out the door leading to the bumpy pavement of the parking lot. "I know it's bright out here, *hon*," I said quickly, opening the ambulance door and reaching under to lift the cot. "We'll be inside soon."

Number Twenty-nine South tried to bring her hands to her face, but the straps held them down. "Just hang on *hon*," I said dryly. "We're almost there."

It was my turn to attend, meaning that my partner would drive the half-mile to the hospital while I tended to the patient. I took a blood pressure cuff and strapped it on her arm while wiping the sweat from my forehead with my shirtsleeve. She was quiet and stared blankly at the bright overhead lights and the rows of compartments along the ambulance walls.

We pulled into the hospital parking lot as I was finishing the report. "We're going in the hospital now," I said quickly, opening the ambulance's rear door and helping my partner pull out the cot. Again I saw her grimace at the light. "We'll be inside in a second, *hon*," I said. We moved through the crowded emergency area and into the bright hallway toward the x-ray department. Twenty-nine South was going to have a routine semi-annual chest x-ray.

My partner and I were friends with most of the x-ray department staff and spent the next several minutes talking and laughing about the current state of emergency medicine while Twenty-nine South lay quietly on her cot against the wall. One of the staff took her to a room. My partner and I went to the lounge for a Coke.

They paged us about an hour later and we found our patient back on our cot in the x-ray waiting area. "Time to go home, *hon*," I said, taking the head of the cot and pulling her back out to the ambulance. We stopped near the exit doors for a few minutes to speak with some other paramedics who had a nursing home patient of their own.

We were about to leave the hospital when I looked out at the bright summer sun hitting the parking lot, causing heat waves to radiate up over the trees. I tried to help my patient by covering her head with a pillowcase. "This will keep the sun off you, hon," I said, looking at the trees and wishing I were fishing instead of moving old people around all day.

My partner held the South Wing door open wide as I pushed the cot hard over the threshold. We stopped at the nurses' station to return the chart. We then moved down the hallway to door Twenty-nine. I pulled the cot next to her bed and waited for my partner to grab the bed pad from the other side. Two quick moves and she was home. I covered her with a sheet and blanket, and was glad that another transport was over. I hoped this would be the last for the day.

My partner grabbed the cot and started back out the door. I followed close behind. My partner was halfway down the hall and I was almost out the door when I heard Twenty-nine South call out.

"Young man!" she called in a voice that seemed out of place coming from her shriveled body. "Young man, I would like a word with you."

I looked at her then down the hall, watching as my partner and the cot disappeared around the corner. Walking to her bedside, I bent over and looked into her gray eyes. "What is it *hon*?" I slowly said.

The woman stretched her skinny arms over the blanket, laying them at her sides. She looked at the dusty ceiling tiles and the row of fluorescent lights, then scanned my uniform. "Please pull up a chair. I wish to tell you something," she said quietly.

I looked out the door and tried to think up a quick excuse to leave. She was probably delirious, many patients were, and I was anxious to leave the stale urine smell of the place.

"This will not take much of your time, young man. I have something to tell you," she said.

On the other side of the room was a battered blue chair that looked left over from the sixties. I brought it to her bedside and hoped this would not take more than a few minutes. Settling down with a plop, I gave Twenty-nine South my best smile, and waited.

She was still staring at the ceiling tiles, her eyes following the intersecting lines spaced exactly eight inches apart. After several seconds of silence, she brought a finger to her mouth and wiped each corner. "My name is not *hon*," she said sternly, not looking away from the eight-inch tiles. "My name is Margaret. You could have checked on my file, if you cared, but it is obvious that you did not."

I smiled weakly and followed her eyes to the ceiling. "I'm sorry, Margaret. It's just that . . ."

"It's just that you didn't *care!*" Margaret paused and rubbed her bony hands over her chest. "You assumed that because I am confined to this bed, in this nursing home, and in this body, that I was not capable or worthy of conversation, other than your patronizing instructions and *annoying* moniker of *hon*. Well, young man, I am confined to this bed. I *do* have a weak body, but my mind is strong, and now *you* are going to listen to *me*."

The smile had left my face. It was replaced with a dry mouth and a tightness in my gut.

"Margaret, if I offended you I am truly . . ."

"All I want from you young man is to listen. That is all. Let me have my words, then you can leave. I expect nothing but your attention for a few minutes. Can you do this?"

I leaned back in the chair, feeling trapped somehow. I wished my partner would come back, but he was probably fixing the cot. "Go ahead, Margaret," I said.

Margaret took a deep breath and blinked several times. "I was born in Germany. It was a small town and you would not recognize the name. The year was 1910 and my family lived in poverty. When I was five my family boarded a ship and came to America. We arrived in New York, and even though it was eighty-five years ago, I can still remember seeing the Statue of Liberty in the harbor. My father eventually took a job in the Detroit auto industry, working for Ford.

"I was the youngest of five children, and the only one to go to college. I attended the University of Michigan and majored in biology. I taught school in Ann Arbor for several years, before getting married and moving up here. My husband took a job with Dow Chemical in Midland, and we settled on a small farm just outside of town.

"By now you are wondering why I am giving you an abbreviated account of my life. There is more, obviously, but it will be enough for my intentions."

I sat up a little and looked at the tiny woman. I was being pulled in two different directions. Part of me wanted to know more about her, and part of me wanted to leave. I sat back against the chair and let her continue.

"I enjoyed the farm life. Growing up in the city, I never experienced the sounds and smells of the country. When I was first married, I would walk for hours in the farm pastures enjoying the wildlife, yet also wishing that I was back teaching biology. But I stayed home and worked at being a good wife. My husband and I never had children. We tried for years, but nothing worked. In those days there wasn't much else to try. My husband died twenty years ago, and my family is now passed on. I am all that is left, except for some distant relatives in Germany whom I never met.

"The reason I tell you all of this young man, is because I wanted you to see me as a person and not just an annoying part of your day. I am a real person, with feelings and hopes and dreams. To you, taking me to the hospital was just a required part of your job. To me, however, it was something I looked forward to. Yes, each day I look forward to an hour, even a minute, away from this place. You see, I have had several strokes and I have lost the use of my body. Every few months they send me for a chest x-ray. It is the only time I can see the world outside this depressing room. Each day I look out the window and watch the sky and hope that a bird might fly by. I do nothing else, really, except eat and mess myself. I want you to know that today you treated me like nothing more than a piece of luggage. You picked me up with callousness and carted me around, totally ignoring my feelings. I will not leave this room for a long time. Perhaps never."

My mouth was dry with a mixture of shame and embarrassment. "Margaret, I . . ."

She held her hand up to stop my apology, waving my words away, but not looking away from the ceiling. "I once had a life and a family and friends. All are gone now, except for my memories. Each day I wish that someone would come and show me the trees or the green farm pastures or even the rain. Do you have a concept of how humiliating it is to be strapped to a hard cot and set aside in a cold hospital hallway, while your attendants ignore your presence and talk of fishing? You made me feel worthless, young man. You made me feel that my life is worth nothing but a few lines on a billing chart."

My neck was now red and swollen. I tried to swallow but my mouth was too dry. I brought a hand to my face and brushed away the tears. "I'm sorry," was all that came out.

"Young man, each day I wonder if it will be my last. Sometimes I have nightmares. Sometimes I wake up crying. Sometimes I wish that death would come. Have you ever wondered what it will be like at the end of your life? I never did when I was young, so I suspect that you don't either. The worst death is that which comes slowly, ebbing along and losing a little strength each day. That is what it is like for me. The nursing staff is mostly caring, although they have little time to spend with me or the other patients.

"I do not ask for an apology. I sense that I have made you feel bad, and that shows that there is compassion within you. I only ask that you treat your patients with respect and understand that no matter how frail or debilitated they may be, they once had a much greater life. They were once like you. Being young, you have the ability to greatly influence the lives of people like me. If you had talked to me about your life, or asked questions about mine, I would have remembered this day for the rest of my remaining life. I would have looked upon this day fondly. You could have helped young man. You could have helped me a great deal."

Margaret closed her eyes and took a long, deep breath. I looked at her skinny face and the tears that ran down her cheeks, matching my own. A nurse came into the room and walked to her side.

"Time for your pills, Margaret," she said.

My partner came to the door with a confused look on his face. He saw that I was upset and shrugged his shoulders. "Come on," he said. "We have another transport on the other side of the building." I left the room as the nurse was helping Margaret with her medication.

After our shift was over, I talked to my partner and explained what had happened. He also felt bad about Margaret and together we came up with some ideas. From that day on, nursing home transports were different. Working as a team, my partner and I viewed each transport as an opportunity to give the patients a special day to remember. Even if they could not communicate, I would talk to them about the day or my life or even sports. With some, I learned enough about their lives to give them a special treat. One old man said that he had been a farmer for many years but now saw nothing of the life he once lived. We gave him a long ambulance ride into the country, parked by a pasture filled with cattle, and opened the rear doors so he could watch the herd. For others we stopped at a local business and bought them ice-cream cones. Sometimes we parked near the school playground and let them watch the children playing.

We would occasionally get into trouble for these extra activities, but looking back, it was worth it. My partner and I started to call these adventures "Margaret runs."

I sent a card with my apology to Margaret, explaining my new way of dealing with patients. I peeked in her room one day while she was sleeping and saw it taped to the wall by her bed. It was one of the last things she read before she died.

RUNNING AWAY

For a brief period in my life, when I must have been mentally unstable, I took up jogging. The words "took up" are probably not the most appropriate since I only survived this new activity for a few days. In a way I was lucky. At least I had the common sense to stop before any damage was done to my body.

My venture into the world of the physically fit was the result of a moderately successful diet. I had spent the better part of a year not eating the foods I really liked while munching on far too many green crunchy things. It seemed only natural to take the next step—getting sweaty for no good reason.

Another reason I chose to abuse my body was that joggers always look so healthy and happy. Think about it. You never see overweight joggers, and runners always appear to be smiling. After much study (and a little experience), I learned that the lack of plump pavement pounders is a result of most people not surviving past day one. And, joggers appear to be happy because their faces are in a constant expression of pain, which is oftentimes confused with a smile.

My first jogging experience, other than running to or away from something, was as a member of Clare's junior high track team. My coach, Mr. Fultz, strongly suggested, in a way that only a coach can, that I limit myself to the shot put. I think he suggested the shot put because it was the only event that required little stamina or forward movement. The problem with practice, however, was that I was required to run one lap around the football field each day for *conditioning*. This presented several problems, the most serious being that by the time I completed my lap, practice was nearly over and I was too exhausted to work on my throwing technique. It was also embarrassing to have the distance runners lap me two or three times before I had finished one complete loop.

My only other jogging experience was in the police academy. Wanting the new cadets to be inspired, the academy administration hired physical conditioning instructors with extraordinarily superior motivational skills. Although I cannot be certain, we cadets assumed these instructors were Marine Corps drill sergeants who were too mean for the military. I found that running myself into convulsions was relatively easy with a two-hundred-pound half-man half-beast screaming in my ear. I probably would have died on the academy track if I didn't know that to these guys, death was not an option.

So I went to the local sporting goods store and wandered into the shoe department, where I studied row after row of athletic footwear. The shoes were stacked on little plastic shelves that went from ground level to nearly out of reach. (This also accurately reflected their prices.) The best shoes, those that were endorsed by a famous sports star and looked like they could jog countless miles on their own, were well into the triple digit range. One pair looked more like a top-secret government experiment than something to put on my feet. I set the shoe gingerly back on the shelf, hoping it was not bruised.

Besides cost, another issue to consider was which style to buy. There were shoes for every conceivable sport and workout activity, but none that were designated for a newborn jogger who didn't want his feet to hurt. Realizing that I needed help, I wandered aimlessly amid the displays until I was spotted by a friendly and knowledge-able salesperson.

His name was Brad. I knew this by reading the black-lettered nameplate pinned to his multi-colored official sales shirt. It was the kind of shirt that somehow fits in a sporting goods store but nowhere else on the planet. Brad was tall and fit and tanned, with a big smile that said he knew it. He glided next to me and paused for a moment to look me over.

"May I help *you?*" he asked.

"Yes, *Brad*," I replied. "I need to buy a pair of jogging shoes."

"Is this a gift for someone?"

I paused before answering, to give myself time to hide the hyphenated phrases churning in my brain and to suck in my gut a little more. "No, *Brad*. It is *I* that needs the shoes," I spit out through my gritted teeth.

"Oh, I see," he said, looking me over once more. "How many . . . *miles* . . . do you cover in a week?"

This, of course, was a difficult question because I had not actu-ally begun my new running lifestyle. Not wanting Brad to think that I was still in the preparatory stage of self-abuse, I averted the truth. Actually, I ran around the backside of the truth, over the foothills of deception, and quite near the mountains of falsehood. "About thirty, *Brad*," I answered. Of course, these were the miles I *drove* in my truck back and forth to work, but my snide and over- confident sales associate hadn't specifically asked for miles *jogged*.

"*Really?*" Brad stammered, with a wrinkled brow. (He looked as if

I had said that I had a part-time job as a body-builder.) "Well now, an avid *jogger* such as you needs top-of-the-line shoes. Come with me."

Brad led me to the far corner of the display, where each shoe was priced more than its weight in gold. He picked up a neon-white shoe with red splashes and held it reverently, as if a genie would appear if he rubbed the sides. "This is the Street-Dancer," he said in a hushed tone. "But, I suppose an avid runner such as yourself is familiar with this product."

I was barely familiar with sweatbands and, until recently, thought that the small swoosh on a large percentage of sporting apparel was a checkmark for quality. But I played along anyway. "Of course," I agreed.

"Here, try them on," Brad said.

Only a custom-tailored suit, or possibly a garment made by NASA, could have a better fit. The shoes wonderfully gripped my feet which, until now, were used to whatever shoes were on sale. Little raised areas inside the shoes pushed against my feet. I felt like I was wearing a rocket launcher. After walking several steps, I felt the difference between the old and the new, and also the cheap and ridiculously expensive. "I'll take them," I said, before I regained my senses.

Brad wrapped the shoes in tissue paper and placed them in a box that was nice enough for Christmas gifts. Before I left the store, he also helped me pick out a new jogging suit. Now properly outfitted, I headed home to begin my self-torture.

My running life began before dawn the following morning. I chose this time of day partly because of the cooler temperature, but mostly because few people would see me in the dark. Armed with my new shoes and jogging outfit, I stepped into the cool dawn air and spent several minutes stretching out leg muscles that had been hibernating for years. After a few deep cleansing breaths, I started down the street in what could only be called a plod. I am certain that a Clydesdale gelding on Valium would have been more graceful—and probably faster.

I thought it would be my lungs that would hurt first, because they had not really been taxed since prom night, but it was my legs that gave me the first pain. Not to be outdone by my lower extremities, my back soon began to throb, followed closely by my feet, even though they were supported by a pair of shoes that cost more than a good set of tires. I probably would have spent more time contemplating whether or not all of this muscle pain was worth the effort, but then my lungs started to burn and keeping them filled with oxygen took all of my mental energy. Still, I might have been proud of my effort, if I was further than four blocks from my home.

I reached a driveway and took the opportunity to walk slowly in a circle. I nearly passed out while sucking in air like a jet engine. Unfortunately, Mitchell, one of the neighborhood children, was standing at the end of the drive.

"You okay, Officer White?" he asked with a concerned and amused voice. "You want a drink of water or something?"

I could have sucked up half the Tobacco River at the moment, but I tried to act nonchalant. "No . . . Mitchell . . . *gasp* . . . I'm . . . *cough* . . . *gag* . . . just fine . . . really," I spit out.

Mitchell followed me down the road as I started for home. Maybe he wanted to see me pass out or perhaps he was just curious. "Hey, Officer White!" he shouted, after I limped along for about a hundred feet. "Nice shoes!"

ONE WHO UNDERSTANDS

H e HAD REACHED THE POINT AT WHICH GUESSING HIS AGE would be difficult, if not altogether impossible; over eighty for sure, perhaps even ninety. He wore old heavy metal-framed glasses, like most men his age seem to wear. They gripped his scalp tightly behind his ears, leaving deep recesses from years of use. A mop of thin hair sat on his head, like gray moss over a weather-beaten log. His wool shirt was dark-blue. I remember that it was wrinkled and buttoned to the top, even in the late August heat. The shirttail was tucked tightly into his brown slacks, which were belted with a thin strip of brown leather midway between his waist and his chest.

It was the way the small trowel shook in his hand that I remember most. He tried to hold it steady against the tremors, but each plunge into the weed-choked ground was awkward and resulted in only a small amount of soil being turned. Undaunted, he continued chipping away at the thick weeds at the headstone's base. I tried to see the name engraved in the tan granite, but could not read it from the driver's seat of my patrol car. Only one name was centered on the small stone. Judging by the undisturbed grass surrounding him and the weathered look of the stone, the person buried here must have passed away long ago.

Behind the man was a flat of colorful flowers, scrubbing tools, and assorted bottles that I assumed were to clean the stone. He worked hard, not looking up at the officer parked near him and not really caring that he was being watched. It was a common scene, actually, and happened often in this quiet cemetery. But something about this man and his hard work moved me. I needed to know more.

He worked there for hours. I know, because I continued driving past on the outside road, looking to see if his old truck was still parked in that quiet corner. At the end of my shift I made one last pass. He was in the process of putting his things in the truck bed. I pulled onto the narrow paved road as he was leaving. For some reason I wanted to speak to him, to at least thank him for cleaning up an old grave, and to hopefully hear his story. He pulled away before I could get close. Not wanting to initiate a traffic stop in a cemetery, especially for no necessary reason, I watched him leave. I did, however, write down the registration plate from the old truck. I was surprised to see that it was from Minnesota.

With the man gone I drove to the grave in the cemetery's quiet corner. It was beautifully restored. The granite was scrubbed clean and the earth around it held lovely flowers with blossoms reaching for the sun from the rich topsoil he, apparently, had brought. Impatiens they were. I know this from my years of growing up on a nursery. Each plant was planted with loving care and watered. He must have loved her, I thought, looking at the name. *Audrey Mae Flowers, born June 6, 1924, died November 11, 1943* it read on the tan stone. *Nineteen years old*, I thought, feeling instantly sad. A daughter? Maybe? A young wife? Possibly. I had to know. I used my unit's radio to call in the plate and waited for the report.

The truck's registration came back to a Willard Johnson out of Saint Paul. *Odd*, I thought, because the registered name didn't match with the name on the stone. I drove back to the department thinking of sending a letter to the man, but I never did.

I looked after the grave in the man's absence. To some this would seem strange, but I pictured him back in St. Paul, many miles away from someone he loved. I never saw him again that summer, or the fall for that matter, but I tended to the flowers, pulling out weeds and keeping things neat until the first hard frost turned his garden to brown leaves and shriveled blossoms.

The following spring the man returned. I didn't see him, but one day while on patrol, and as usual checking the grave, I found the earth dug fresh and again, a flat of colorful impatiens planted around the stone. He must have come at a different time of day, or perhaps on my day off. I was disappointed to have missed him.

Again that summer I took care of the grave. Sometimes I drove by after work and pulled the weeds, and even carried a bucket of water for the flowers. He would have been pleased to know that his special grave was being maintained.

It was late in the spring of the following year when I saw the man again. He was driving a rental car this time, but his shape, as he knelt over the grave, was unmistakable. He looked older, if that were possible. The shaking in his hands was more pronounced and he was wearing a thick wool sweater even though it was a warm day. As before, behind him was a flat of impatiens and scrubbing tools. Driving closer in my unit, I prepared to meet him.

"Good morning, Officer," he said slowly, his voice raspy with labored breathing. "Nice day, isn't it?" He held the spade in his right hand and tried to control the shaking. He was unsuccessful, so finally he rested it against his leg to hide the tremors.

"I wanted to thank you for your work, sir. For the past two years, and now the third, you have made this corner of the cemetery more beautiful."

The man looked up at me, studying my uniform and polished badge before looking back at the grave. "Thank you," he said slowly. He ran his hand over the polished stone, tracing the name with his fingertips. "I loved her," he said, moving his hand back to the ground and pulling out a tall weed.

"I see by your license plate that you are from Minnesota. When did you live in Michigan?"

The old man smiled slightly and moved the trowel back to the stone, carefully scraping some small weeds away from the base, the blade making a high-pitched whine. "Until three years ago I never set foot in your state." He began working harder in the soil, turning over the ground so it would be ready for the flowers.

I had to know. Really I did. He seemed like the kind of man that enjoyed leaving me with many questions. And he did. Questions that swirled around in the spring air, demanding to be answered. After two years of tending the grave in his absence I somehow felt that I had a right to know, or at least deserved an opportunity to understand. "She must have been someone very special. It's a shame she died so young," I said, hoping he would tell me the story. It was a story that I needed to hear.

"My great grandson found her. I still don't exactly understand how, having no experience with computers and this thing called the Internet. But, he and his computer seem connected to the world and I asked for his help. It only took a few weeks. Funny, isn't it? I search for years through public records and the kid finds her in less than a month." He paused and set the trowel on the ground before turning and sitting back, facing me.

"Was she . . ."

"No, she was not my wife. I can see you are interested, or at least confused, as I would be seeing an old man hunched over a small grave a thousand miles from his home."

"I'm sorry, sir. I don't mean to pry. It's just . . ."

"We met in California, way up in the north where I was stationed in the army. Audrey was just out of high school and working at a small café near my base. Some would call it love at first sight, although that seems a little trite." He picked a plant from the plastic tray and pushed it into a shallow hole. "She was a volunteer nurse's aide at our base hospital," he said, pushing dirt around the plant. "I was in a line of men waiting for my vaccination for my deployment overseas. I remember thinking at the time that I had never seen anyone as beautiful as Audrey." He paused when he said her name and his face drooped with its mentioning. "She was tall, much taller than most girls I knew. At nearly six feet she looked me squarely in my eyes. It was her smile that I fell in love with. She walked by the line of men handing out small packages of something or other and when she came to me our hands touched briefly." The man reached for another plant. He looked at me not like a grandfather, but as another man. "Do you understand what a simple touch from a special woman can do, young man?" he asked.

I looked at the tan stone and the neatly carved name on the front, then to the growing line of bright flowers planted at its base. "Yes," I answered.

"I guessed that you would. You must or you would not be here talking to an old man planting flowers for someone he knew for only a few days."

"What happened?"

The man absently smoothed the dark earth around the last plant and looked at the stone. "I had a pass for the next few days before my company shipped out. Each and every hour was spent with Audrey. Most of the time we just talked. I had never met anyone like her. We finished each other's sentences and I swear we could read each other's minds. I was far too young to understand how rare that was. I would look at her and shake my head, almost not believing how lucky it was that we had found each other. By the last day we knew what real love was. Not a love like in the movies, or even in most marriages. I mean true love. I could not imagine her not being a part of my life."

"Your soul mate," I said quietly.

"That seems to be the correct phrase young man." He ran his fingers over the base of the grave. "She was the mate for my soul, and she never left. I would have married her that last day, but we decided to wait until I returned stateside. We exchanged addresses and I left for France knowing that we would always be together."

I wanted to hear the rest of the story, but stopped from asking the final questions. Somehow I knew that if I waited he would continue.

"Four years later I was back in the states. I had a thirty-day leave and headed for California. I assumed the reason that I received no letters was because of the war. I was wrong." He looked to the sky through the maples and nearly smiled. "After I left the base there was an outbreak of influenza. Working in the hospital she contracted the disease. Audrey was dead before I reached the beach at Normandy. I wanted to visit her grave but was told that her body was shipped back home. The problem was that I never knew where her real home was. No one could give me any information. It was only three years ago that I found her, with the help of my great grandson."

I looked down at the ground and the bright flowers, not knowing what to say next.

"Don't be sorry for me, young man. I had a good life. I married several years later and had four wonderful children. I loved my wife with all my heart, but I never forgot Audrey. My wife knew all about her, and this may sound strange, even she felt a certain loss. She understood there was a part of my heart that would always be with Audrey. My wife passed away ten years ago and now I live near my children. In case you are wondering, I also work very hard to keep my wife's grave like this."

"Will you be coming back next year?" I quickly asked, before considering his age.

"I have no idea, young man. At my age a year is a long time and much can happen."

I helped the man pick up the empty tray and his tools, loading them in the back of the rental car. His last words to me were, "You are one who understands. That is good."

By the summer of the following year, he had not returned to the quiet corner of the cemetery. Weeds had grown up along the stone and I knew that he would never be back. That night after work I bought a flat of flowers and borrowed some tools. I do this each year now, because I understand.

A MANLY PAUSE

JEFF FOXWORTHY, A COMEDIAN WITH THE SOUTHERN DRAWL JUST raspy enough to be catchy, created a wonderful routine based on his colorful descriptions of rednecks. His, "You might be a redneck if . . ." questions have entertained audiences of all social backgrounds, and all colors of necks. My all-time favorite is, "If your momma keeps a spit cup on the ironing board, you might be a redneck."

There are hundreds more, but from my years of law enforcement experience, I have one that Jeff seems to have missed. My contribution to the redneck hall of fame is, "If you've ever been to a wedding reception where the police were called to break up a fight between the bride and maid of honor, you might be a redneck." Okay Jeff, you are free to use this one in your act.

It all started on one of those drizzly late-March days in Michigan, when Mother Nature is trying to decide whether to go ahead and let spring arrive or just punish the state for awhile longer. Saturday morning dawned with gray rainy skies, followed by more gray rainy skies and, by evening, some harder rain for no good reason. Any part of the landscape that was not depressing brown snow or depressing brown grass was oozing cold depressing brown mud. The large snow-banks that struggled to survive the rain stood slumped in defeat, like dirty groups of filthy, listless sheep. Dark puddles dotted everything that was not already muddy, reflecting the tormented slate-gray sky. It was obvious that Mother Nature had chosen the punishment alternative.

The marriage of Pam and John did not exactly shake the rafters of our community, or even move the blinds, for that matter. After all, they had been living together for many years and had three small children. They lived in a tiny turquoise and rust colored trailer that, on most days, would pass a building inspection provided the inspector was in a good mood. What *did* surprise the community was the elaborate wedding that they had planned. It seemed as if they were trying to have the wedding of their dreams, which should have taken place eight years, one trailer and three children earlier.

As a result eight, count them, eight bridesmaids and groomsmen donned rented clothing that was so foreign to them it looked like they were playing dress-up instead of certifying the love of their friends. (I found out later that the men's cummerbunds spawned nearly fifty jokes and off-hand comments, none of which can be mentioned in this book.)

Pam and John were married at one of the local churches to the relief of many, especially their children. It is always a special event when mom marries dad. Unfortunately the celebration of their union had begun earlier that morning. By the time the couple said "I do" both had consumed enough alcohol to drive an Oldsmobile across the continent. This fact was not unnoticed by the minister who, understanding the possible consequences, hurried through the service and left before any more of the wedding party vomited.

The boisterous group hung around the church for awhile, before realizing that they could adjourn to the hall so the *real* party could begin. And it was this *real* party that caused my unintended invitation to the blessed nuptial.

Although it was difficult to sort out the many different versions of the event, it seems the original argument began when the bride's mother accused the best man of not ordering enough kegs of beer. The two squared off like World Wrestling Federation fighters with angry eyes and slurred speech. I was later told that Pam's mother went through the entire gambit of four-letter hyphenated words without ever taking the Marlboro from her lips. Foxworthy would have been proud.

From this point the details are sketchy, but Pam did defend her mother, as only an intoxicated bride can, by taking a folding chair and knocking the best man silly. Not willing to stand by while her husband writhed on the dusty floor of the rented hall, the best man's wife, and also the maid of honor, retaliated by drenching the bride with a quart of cheap beer. Within moments the two were locked up like snarling cats, overturning tables and any guests that happened to be in the vicinity. One of the younger nephews called 911 while the rest of the bridal party moved into fighting stances and the guests chose sides.

As any police officer will tell you, mixing alcohol and relatives is never a good idea, even under the best of circumstances. Combining large quantities of firewater at a gathering such as this can produce altercations of epic proportions. And it was these epic proportions that were relayed over my radio that night.

I was working alone and immediately called for backup, as was department policy and common sense. Luckily several units from surrounding counties were available to help. We met at a location about a block away from the reception before driving into the hall parking lot in one long string of police blue. When I pulled into the parking lot in the lead car, I remember thinking that I should have called for more help, like the Michigan National Guard.

What I saw on that dreary late-March night was not a *single* fight, but an entire parking lot filled with individual fights scattered among the withering snow piles and slush-filled puddles. Under the blue handicapped parking sign the bride and maid of honor rolled on the slick pavement. The bride's white gown and the maid's maroon dress were now intertwined, making them look like a giant lumpy candy cane. The bride's mother was trying to disembowel one of the groomsmen with a pool cue by the front door. Over by the black and rust van, that was to be the honeymoon vehicle, the groom's uncle was pounding on a tuxedo-clad usher. Several other fights were in various stages of completion around the rest of the parking lot.

My first problem was trying to decide where to start. Thinking quickly, I activated my unit's siren, thinking the group would realize that the law had arrived. They did, but instead of stopping their pummeling, they sped up in earnest. Like some grainy scene from a Keystone Cop movie we separated and tried to stop the carnage. Some of the fighting teams broke up easily with a simple shove and stern look, while others required more *direct* methods. I had stopped two fights myself and assisted in the arrest of several others under the local ordinance for disorderly conduct, when I looked back to the center of the lot and saw that two of my fellow officers were in trouble.

One of the larger groomsmen was refusing to stop his assault on an equally large guest, even with two officers pulling at them. I jumped into the brawl, in an attempt to arrest both persons. At times it was difficult to tell who was winning the fight. All five of us moved together like a swinging pile of anger. I swung, they swung back, my brother officers swung into the pile with each of us never sure if we would connect with friend or foe. Each time I tried to handcuff one of the fighters, he would break free and hit my buddies or me. I looked across the lot at the other officers for help, but they were equally busy with fights of their own. Just as I was considering calling time, hoping we could all rest for sixty seconds and get our breath, she ran out the front door.

She was the youngest and most attractive of the bridesmaids who, until now, had been content to stay inside and let the silly boys fight it out. The problem was that her boyfriend happened to be one of the largeness twins we were trying to arrest. With a shriek only possible from a twenty-one-year-old who had just stood in her first wedding and drank *way* too many whiskey sours, she ran across the parking lot in her black spiked heels and puffy maroon gown toward us. What happened next was a study in instinctive male reaction.

I watched her staggering toward us and braced myself for her to jump on my back. She was screaming for us to leave her man alone, when she hit the ice. With a total lack of grace, she went airborne, landing squarely on her back in a rather sloppy slush-filled puddle. This resulted in one of her legs pointing due north and the other pointing due south. Her gown fell around her chest like a maroon throw rug, exposing the only thing between her and the Lord, which was a pair of lacy pink panties. This resulted in the ultimate crotch-shot. Suddenly, as if by some inborn cue that all men share, even in the most hostile and competitive of circumstances, we stopped. I stopped trying to handcuff my guy. The other officers stopped swinging. The groomsman and guests stopped fighting back. We all stared at the puddle and what was pointing in each direction. In a few seconds the girl recovered her senses and struggled to her feet. Then, with the sudden realization that the show was over, we resumed our activities.

Moments later more officers arrived and the brawl was over. In all we arrested four of the bridal party and three guests. By the time we pulled out of the parking lot, the remaining seventy-five percent of the bridal party was back in the hall nursing their wounds with the remaining beer.

SOONER OR LATER

"You know . . . Al . . . I don't mind the pounding rain. Really, I don't. I can even take the near hurricane-force wind that is blowing it sideways over the highway." Ken leaned toward me and raised his voice for effect. "But we've just been passed by a %#&@$%# tree!" He leaned forward in his seat and tightly gripped the dashboard, watching the twenty or so feet of visible road in front of my truck for other skidding and flying plant life. Even in the dim light cast by the instrument panel I could see the whiteness of his knuckles. Being the friend that I am, I tried to calm my buddy.

"It was more like a large branch."

Ken gave me his best patronizing grimace. "I've built tree forts in smaller ones," he shouted over the roar of the storm. "Don't you think it might be a good idea to pull over for a while? Like in a bomb shelter?"

"I will admit that the storm's a little strong."

"A *little* strong! Hurricane Hugo was a *little* strong! This is crazy!"

"Oh, we'll be fine. Besides, Mark will worry about us if we show up late."

"*I'm* worried about us!" Ken screamed, leaning back and tightening his seat belt.

169

It was true that the storm was a dandy, perhaps *bordering* on typhoon strength, but not yet strong enough to slow this adventure. That would take a tornado. A big one.

For as long as I care to remember Mark, Ken, and me have been partners for the opening of Michigan's duck season. Normally we spend the first week of the season relatively close to home, camping beside our favorite marsh, sharing in good male fellowship, and *not* killing ducks. This year was different because of Mark's profound statement, "Hey guys, if we are going to camp and not kill ducks, why don't we camp and *not* kill them way up in the Upper Peninsula?"

I still don't understand why it seemed that Mark's idea made so much sense. It may have been because Mark always seemed to *make* sense, at least compared to some of Ken's and my ideas. And Mark, as always, had worked on his idea for some time before thrusting it on us one evening over a poker game. He talked about the adventure between hands of the entire game. Even as the last hand was dealt, he kept up his enthusiasm.

"I fished there last summer," he said, while dealing out five cards to each of us. "The cabins are pretty rustic, but clean, and we'll have a great view of the river. The old guy that runs the place says ducks are always flying around in the fall."

"Was this *before* or *after* you showed interest in renting a cabin in October?" Ken asked, throwing two chips in the center of the table.

"That's not important!" Mark shot back. "Besides, the number of ducks never stopped us from having a good time."

"Sounds like fun," I said, folding my hand and admiring the pile of chips in front of Mark. "Besides, I'm ready for a good road trip."

"Me, too," Ken said, tossing his cards to the center of the table. "Perhaps it will help my poker game."

We began making plans that evening. Mark, as always, made a list of necessary items, including way too much food and beverages. He was able to get off work earlier than Ken and me, but he had to leave toward the end of the week, which required us to drive separately. Because of this, Mark made it to the right-hand side of the Upper Peninsula hours ahead of Ken and me, and hours before the storm.

The flashing road sign in the distance could mean only one of two things; either the Mackinaw Bridge was closed or an escort would be necessary to cross the mighty span. Moving closer, we found the latter was the reason. Ken looked at the backed-up traffic and ran his hands through his thinning hair. "You probably heard that a car went over the bridge several years ago on a night like this. One of those little foreign jobs. They said the wind came up through the grates and just pushed it over the guardrails." He paused for a moment and cracked his knuckles. "How much does your truck weigh?" he asked.

"Enough, buddy," I said calmly. "Don't worry, in an hour we will be in camp."

Because of the escort rule, we had to wait until a bridge authority vehicle could lead us across. This meant that we would follow the vehicle over the five miles of suspension bridge at about twenty miles an hour. Once we began traveling over the water, it was easy to see why the precautions were necessary. Huge drafts of wind shot though the open grates of the bridge and shook my truck like a Matchbox car. Rain streamed down in angry torrents, making visibility almost nonexistent. Nearly a half-hour later we reached the Upper Peninsula. Gusts of wind swirled rain on the black, slick roads. Leaves and small tree branches littered the highway as we slowly moved northeast.

Called "The Camp," by locals, our destination consisted of eight small cabins along the narrow North Channel of Lake Huron that separated the mainland from Neebish Island. Each cabin was covered in asphalt siding with a brown brick pattern, common in the thirties and forties, when they were probably built.

Camps such as this once dotted Michigan's Upper Peninsula at prime fishing spots, before motor homes, reliable camping equipment, and the big bridge. Before the Mackinaw Bridge was built, downstate fishermen, as well as hunters, waited in long lines each summer and fall to cross the straits on car ferries. At least some of the camps are still used and have changed little. The Camp's cabins looked just like the photos in my grandparent's album, except now I was looking at them through a torrential rain and in the darkness of night.

We pulled in front of cabin five and saw Mark moving to the door. He was wearing his stupid multicolored poker hat and a gray sweat suit. He pushed the door open, staying back from the falling rain. "Buddies!" he shouted over the storm. "Welcome home, friends."

Ken and I slogged through the mud and brought in our gear, taking time to kid Mark about not helping us and for not being worried that we were washed over the bridge.

"Oh, I knew Al would drive through anything to not kill ducks. Heck, a little rain won't stop a real *Alaska man*, right?"

"Maybe not, but it was the tree that nearly stopped the Alaska man's truck," Ken said, setting down the last of his gear and looking around the tiny cabin.

Although from the outside the cabin looked like a throwback to the Great Depression, the inside had been re-modeled sometime around the sixties. The plaster walls were painted in turquoise, with bright pink and blue plastic fish and birds hanging on far-too-large nails. Multi-colored shag carpeting covered the creaking wooden floor, except near the door where it was worn to the plywood beneath. An old, rounded refrigerator sat next to some orange cupboards on the far wall. In the center of the room was a round table covered with a faded flower-print plastic cover. Two bedrooms without doors each held a single bed that sloped toward the center. Because of the old fuel oil furnace, the cabin smelled like burnt dust. Ken tossed his hat on the table and looked at Mark.

"This is perfect!" Ken shouted. "I was worried that we might become soft staying in a modern, or at least comfortable, place. What a wonderful place to stay while not shooting ducks."

Mark beamed and spread his arms wide, reverently. "And the best part is that the bathrooms in the building across the drive aren't working! Because of all the rain, the septic system is flooded. This is going to be just like our old camp. We get to use the woods behind the cabin!"

"Cool," I said, noticing that it was actually raining harder.

Ken began moving gear off an orange vinyl couch in order to check the relic for softness. "I'll sleep here," he said. "That way, when the water in the driveway comes in through the door, I can let you guys know."

I awoke at dawn and stumbled out of my bed and into the main room of the cabin. I padded to the window over the sink and looked out across the channel. It was about a mile wide and I could just see Neebish Island and the hills beyond. Over the faded blue water hung low clouds with shards of sunrise lighting them in streaks that touched the lapping waves. A giant freighter came down the channel from the north; its giant shape made the waterway suddenly look small. Mark came in from the back door and walked to my side.

"Okay, here are the rules," he said. "I get the big oak right outside the door. You can have the small maple clump next to it and Ken, because he is the last one up, gets the thorn apple." Mark paused for a second, looking over at Ken still sleeping on the couch. "That should make things interesting."

"I heard that," Ken said from under his sleeping bag.

We ate a quick breakfast and went outside to check on the boat. The camp owner promised that he had a worthy watercraft we could use for hunting. We sloshed across the flooded lawn near the cabin and down the mud path toward the docks. The docks themselves were just several worn planks suspended above the river by rusty steel tubes. They looked about as sturdy as my last tree house. Each board creaked under us as we walked away from the wet shore and over the very wet channel. Tied to the far plank was a sixteen-foot aluminum boat with an ancient motor. Ken was impressed.

"Oh good, it leaks," he said. "I was hoping we would be wet the entire trip and not just on the way up here."

Mark looked at the two feet of water gently rocking inside the boat. "It's from all the rain, dummy," he said. "We just need some buckets to bail her out."

"Actually, she does leak a little." We turned around to see an old man approaching us on the dock.

"John!" Mark shouted. He walked toward the man and shook his hand vigorously. "My buddies got in late last night. Something about a little rain held them up."

John was wearing an old pair of bib overalls and a Ford baseball cap. He looked like someone who spent most of his time working on old tractors when he wasn't renting tiny cabins to crazy duck hunters. He followed Mark back to the boat and kicked at the motor with a brown work boot that was older than me. "Had the motor going last week," he said as if talking about a long lost friend. "Ran pretty good, I guess. You will still need to bail the boat out each morning before your hunt. Once, of course, you take care of the rain water."

"Good," Ken said. "By the way, John, where does one hunt ducks around here?"

John looked across the channel, put his hands in his pockets and took a deep breath. He had the same look as the old farmer that once let me hunt deer on his place; like he was sharing a big secret. "Look a little north across the channel," he nearly whispered. "See that brown-green over there? *Cattails.* The place is called Jones Bay. Don't know why. Ain't never been any Jones's around here. Anyway, *sooner or later,* everyone hunts Jones bay for ducks."

"What about the freighters? We saw one this morning," I asked.

"Oh, they can't come into the bay. Too shallow, you know. They stay on the channel."

"I gathered that, John. My question revolves around the fact that we must cross the channel to get to the bay."

"Oh yeah. Well, you just look *real good* to the north and don't try to cross until they are by you. You should probably look to the south, too. Sometimes they come that way."

I briefly considered the consequences of boating in the center of the channel and being approached by a ship the size of my hometown subdivision. The wake alone could capsize a boat like this. Even one that didn't leak.

We went back to the cabin and changed into marsh-scouting clothes, and grabbed some buckets to empty the boat. Back at the dock, Mark worked on the motor while Ken and I bailed out enough water to start a cranberry bog. We had most of the water out when Mark got the motor running. It sounded like a washing machine full of road gravel and covered us in a thick cloud of blue-black smoke.

"Runs a little rough," Mark said, closing the top and adjusting the throttle. He shut the cover carefully, as if not to knock loose any working parts of the motor.

"This thing burn wet grass, or what?" Ken shouted over the rumbling engine.

"Let's just head across the channel before she quits," Mark suggested.

I considered Mark's statement for a moment, taking into consideration that he has always been the most practical of us three. "Right! That way we can be in the middle of the shipping lane before it stops, rather than safely at the dock." Mark looked at Ken, then to me.

"We have oars, you know."

I looked at the battered, cracked oars lying in the boat. "Oh, I guess we are *safe* then," I answered.

As we drifted away from the dock, the motor actually began to run better and only left the smoke trail of a fighter jet. Mark headed toward the center of the channel, taking time at my insistence to look for any approaching freighters. After a mile we were once again in relatively shallow water and approaching the bay. The green-brown cattails moved with the breeze and created calm pockets of water that appeared perfect for ducks. Everywhere we looked, we saw wonderful places to hunt.

"Maybe this won't be so bad," Ken said, looking at a promising clump of cattails. He directed us into a quiet cove and found that the thick vegetation would conceal the boat and give us a good spot to hunt. "Let's come to this spot in the morning," he said, after we were in position.

Normally I wake on opening morning of duck season to a stiff back from a tent or camper bed and the coldness of early October all around me. This year it was to the heat of a comfortable cabin and a wonderfully soft bed. Even with the blaring alarm clock, I longed for a few more minutes of sleep and snuggled deeper under the blankets. I drifted off until moments later, when Ken kicked my bed.

"Rise and shine, buddy," Ken called out. He was already dressed and headed out to his thorn apple bush. Mark was up too, putting together some sandwiches for the hunt.

It took two trips to the boat to load our gear and another several minutes for Mark to get the motor started. As we pulled away from the dock, I looked to the north at a tight grouping of stars. Moments later I noticed the stars were moving rapidly toward our little boat. "Back to the dock!" I shouted from the front of the boat.

"What?" Mark yelled over the grinding motor.

"Freighter!" I screamed, while pointing at the moving lights.

Mark and Ken looked at my artificial constellation then took the time to panic. I grabbed the side of the boat and held on while Mark made a sharp U-turn and headed for the dock. We held the rough boards as the freighter drifted past, sending large waves crashing against the dock.

"That was close," Ken said, quietly. He pulled his hat down tighter on his head then looked at his watch. "We better hurry. It's nearly duck hunting time."

I had temporarily forgotten about duck hunting. I looked to the east and saw that the sky was beginning to lighten. Mark pulled away from the dock once more, checked for oncoming ships, and then sped across the channel to Jones Bay. After several minutes of being lost, we found the cattails from the day before and prepared for dawn and the first flight of ducks.

We didn't have long to wait, for dawn, that is. Gray light smeared across the bay, pushing away the darkness and bringing with it total silence. Always before on opening day, even in the worst years, there had been the whistling of duck wings overhead as they left the marsh before regulation shooting hours. Above us was only quiet and the rustling of cattails being tossed by a slight breeze. Still, we were hopeful. After all, we had a big bay with terrific duck habitat to ourselves. It just meant some patient waiting.

Our patience lasted for about twenty minutes into shooting hours, then turned to impatient expectations of time. We sat solemnly in the boat, looking at the duckless sky and absently shredding cattails until we saw the smokestack. Ken noticed it first and motioned toward it with his right thumb.

"This is your fault, Mark," he said looking at the freighter's tallest point. A couple hundred feet away a giant ship cruised past our blind mostly hidden by the cattails. "We could have been back near Houghton Lake in our own blind, *not* shooting ducks that would have at least had the courtesy to fly over once in a while."

The freighter was nearly out of sight when its wake hit us. Although muffled by the cattails, it still rocked our tiny boat, causing us to hold on to the rails tightly.

We sat there all morning without seeing one duck. After the last of Mark's rather good sandwiches were gone, he began rummaging around in the rear of the boat. Taking a box from under the seat, he started unfolding what looked like a wrinkled heavy raincoat. "What in the world are you doing?" Ken asked, pausing and looking at me for a moment. "With all that noise you will scare the ducks away." Ken grinned and looked at the empty sky.

"Float tube," Mark said, as if we should have known.

"Abandoning ship?" I asked.

"You know, Mark, I was only kidding about it being all your fault. Well, mostly kidding. Anyway, you don't have to leave," Ken offered.

Mark pretended to ignore us. "Got this thing at a Duck's Unlimited raffle. I figured that since we are not seeing ducks in the air, they may be hiding in the cattail pockets."

"So," Ken said slowly, "you are going to float around and herd them toward the boat like feathered cattle?"

Mark smiled and began blowing into a tiny valve on the tube. "I can move silently though the cattails and get some jump shots. At least we may have duck to eat tonight," Mark said between breaths.

For the next hour Mark did little talking because all his energy was spent blowing up the float tube. When he became light-headed, he would stop and put his finger over the valve and smile at us. With little else to do, Ken and I spent the time watching as Mark blew red-faced into the tube and offering encouragement to our friend.

"Blow harder, Mark," Ken shouted at one point, causing Mark to lose concentration and also lose a sizable amount of air in the tube.

"Bet you wish that you played the tuba in band, huh?" I offered.

"You guys want to help?" he asked.

I looked at Ken, then back to Mark. "No, we are just here for moral support," I said.

When the tube was fully inflated Mark began packing supplies into several pockets around the sides. He put in a box of shotgun shells, a bottle of water and some rope. Ken and I watched as he set it over the side of the boat and prepared to get in. We had to lean back to counter the weight of Mark going over the front. Ken held Mark's shotgun as he sort of fell into the tube while hanging desperately onto the boat's rail. He let go of the boat and drifted a few inches away before holding out his hand for his gun. Ken handed it to him gently and Mark was underway.

For a moment I felt almost envious of Mark for having something else to do besides sitting and not seeing ducks. This period of envy was short-lived, however, as Mark began frantically kicking back to the boat. "Help!" he shouted.

Ken and I watched as Mark, and the float tube around his waist, began to sink into the deep waters of Jones Bay. Having never been in the tube before, Mark failed to calculate the tube's flotation properties against his and his equipment's weight. This resulted in our friend looking like a giant bobber being pulled under by a supernatural bass. By the time Mark was back at the boat, his waders were filled with water and the only thing that was dry was his shotgun, which he held over his head like a great-plains warrior after a battle.

We helped him back in the boat and offered our advice and encouragement. "Interesting plan of attack," Ken said. "I never would have thought of stalking ducks from *under* the water."

Mark didn't say much for awhile and spent most of the time letting the air out of the tube, and shivering.

When Mark began turning blue we began our trip back to the cabin. Arriving at the dock, John was waiting for us. He stood holding a piling and smiled broadly.

"Well, how did you boys do?" he asked, pulling our boat next to the dock.

I was the first to respond. "I thought you said that sooner or later everyone hunts Jones Bay."

John smiled and looked across the river. "Sure did. No one ever shoots ducks over there, but they all give it a try."

That night after dinner and long after the first poker hand was dealt, Ken summed up the trip perfectly. "Well, boys," he said. "At least we are too far from home to go back to work."

FLUSH WITH PRIDE

LIKE ALL BAD THINGS IT HAPPENED WITHOUT WARNING. MY WIFE'S tone of voice indicating that all was not well in the basement started the whole event. The seriousness of the tone was somewhere between her discovering a large garter snake under the juniper bush and finding, once again, that our Labrador had gone on a trash-dumping spree. Yet something was different in her voice this time. A quiet, intense urgency accompanied her, "You'd better get down here." I rushed down the stairs with the knowledge that whatever awaited me was not going to be pleasant, and it would be my fault.

Water may be the one thing that all life needs to survive, but when it is bubbling up from a floor drain and oozing across your basement floor, it is difficult to appreciate its place in the universe. "Spill something?" I offered, with my signature grin. My wife was not amused by my attempt at humor. In fact, the look she gave me made me wish I had said something different like, "Where do we keep the life jackets?"

Until today I was only vaguely aware that we *had* a floor drain. It had rested in the cement floor, dormant, until becoming active for today's surprise eruption. No problem, I thought, stuffing a towel down the hole and packing it tightly. I reveled in my ingenuity only for a minute, until the downstairs toilet began to overflow. This was my clue that my first real test as a new homeowner was well underway.

Like all the other home-related problems that had come up since I acquired a mortgage, I consulted my friend and confidant, Ken, who lived across the street. Ken, who has far more experience in domestic matters of *all types*, was very supportive, in his own way.

"And you thought that stuffing a towel down the hole would solve the problem?" he cackled.

Once Ken was able to speak without breaking into fits of laughter, he pointed reverently across the road to my house.

"You, my friend, have a backed-up septic system. Your tank probably needs to be pumped. When was the last time you had it cleaned out?"

"Well, I ah . . . they need to be pumped, huh?"

Ken smiled and slowly shook his head back and forth. "Where's your tank? We'll go take a look."

"It's right in . . . the yard . . . somewhere."

"You *don't know* where your septic tank is? Where did you think all that stuff went? In the river?" Ken was enjoying my helplessness.

"Look, I've never lived in the country, *okay*! I didn't know to ask about septic locations when I bought the place. Now, where would I look for the thing?"

"You know that large part of your yard that is always green, even in August? Well, your tank will be between that and your house."

"That's about a half-acre!" I cried.

"Give or take a little. The tank should be about a foot underground, or so you hope. If I didn't have to work today I would stay and help you dig."

∼

My experience in the landscaping business, now known as the dark years, prepared me for many things, the most important of which was the knowledge that I should never run a business, and the least of which was how to operate a shovel. I really didn't mind all the digging. After all, it was a nice summer day, with a cool breeze and a mild temperature. Oh sure, it would have been nice to know, even remotely, where my septic tank was, but I tried to convince myself to see this as an adventure. Besides, the neighbors were quite interested in my activities.

I quickly found that nothing brings neighbors together like a good old-fashioned plugged-up septic system. Before long, two of my neighbors were standing beside me, trying to remember where the previous owners had installed the tank. I dug in each place they pointed, but found nothing but dirt. They also had their favorite septic horror stories, each of which went something like this.

"There I was, at two in the morning on a bitter cold night. Not some blue-bird day like this. I'm talking real cold here. And, I was not afraid to go outside and check the tank, either. You have no idea how easy it is for you kids...."

By the time my helpful neighbors left, my front yard looked like Serbia after a bomber strafing run. The only one who seemed to thoroughly enjoy this adventure was my Labrador, Taku. Having the mind of a breadstick, Taku viewed each new mound of dirt as his personal throne. That is, he sat on them and then he peed on them. It was also difficult to get the dog to understand the concept that it was okay for *me* to dig in the yard, but not for him. About every tenth shovel full or so, I would see him watching me as if to say, "Hey, I got swatted for the same thing last week!" Taku released his frustrations by digging additional holes whenever I was not looking.

After several hours of intense yard assault, I located the tank. At least I thought it was the tank. It was large and made of cement.

Of course, it is one thing to find your tank, and yet another to locate the lid. Before long I had excavated several yards of soil and still could not find an opening. Even though I tried to pretend that I was a famous archeologist in Egypt searching for the opening to a lost tomb, I could not get excited about the treasure that lay uncovered.

About a half-hour later I located the lid. After prying it open with my shovel handle I found, in fact, that my tank needed pumping. As if by cue, several of my neighbors returned to witness the unveiling.

"Yup, she's full all right," said one.

"Full to the rim," said another.

In a way, I felt violated. After all, this was kind of a private matter. But, looking at this incident as a whole, it was sort of good for me. After all, it's kind of humbling to stare into the open hole of your septic tank. A person could be the most powerful man on earth, but when his septic tank is open, he is just a man.

Each neighbor had an opinion about who to call for the pumping process. Each of their candidates was rated on speed, power, and ability to assess problems. They were still arguing over who was best as they walked away to their homes. In the end, I looked in the yellow pages and picked the one with the biggest ad.

Now, all I had to do was wait. The owner said he was very busy, being summer and all, with the increase in cabin owners. He talked on and on. I learned more about the plight of septic tank pumpers from this phone conversation than I really wanted to know. I began to feel sorry for bothering him with my little problem.

I passed the time waiting for my plumbing rescue by sitting atop a dirt pile and yelling at the dog. Several of my other neighbors drove past and shouted words of encouragement.

"Hey, Al, interesting landscape design," one said.

"What are you doing, Al, fishing for brown trout?" quipped another.

So, I sat atop my dirt mount, hoping that when the truck arrived it would not be noticed by too many people. Unfortunately, there is a certain degree of embarrassment involved with these problems, even though all rural dwellers have, at one time or another, sat on their own mounds awaiting the pump truck. My hope of anonymity was smashed, however, when I heard the distant rumble and grinding of a stick shift.

Rounding my corner with considerably more speed than necessary was my nightmare of what a septic pump truck might be. The truck was older than me, by several years, and was painted fire hydrant red. There might have been an exhaust system on the beast, but there was no actual connection with the engine. It looked like a giant version of the Tonka trucks I played with as a kid, with a bright red coffee can attached to the back. Contrasting nicely with the please-notice-me red paint, were huge white letters spelling *SEPTIC SUCCESS*. Below the company name was a smaller sentence, about the size of a compact car, that read, *IF YOU CAN PASS IT, WE CAN PUMP IT*. I have seen billboards that were smaller than the moving hulk of advertising space that pulled into my driveway. The only thing missing was a flashing light bar over the cab and a piercing siren.

The driver climbed down from the cab with a confidence only possible from a man who had seen his share of toilet turmoil. I tried to introduce myself, but he brushed past like an experienced trauma surgeon arriving at the scene of a horrific traffic accident.

"How long has she been like this?" he asked, placing his hands on his hips and staring into the blackness of my tank. This is the same look my doctor gives me when asking how long I have been at this weight. "Probably don't give her much thought, do you? Just flush and forget, right?"

Before I could answer, he walked back to the truck and began unrolling a hose the size of an elephant trunk. At this point a large pod of neighborhood children arrived on bikes, filling my driveway with spoked wheels and inquisitive smiles. I did my best to ignore them, but they were soon crowded around me and my dirt piles. Septic Ted was now clamping sections of the hose together with practiced efficiency. Now don't get me wrong. I love children. I work with children all day, nearly every day. I have made great sacrifices for the children of Clare. I would do anything to help a child. It's just that at this particular moment I did not want anyone, especially a child, near my house and my septic problems.

"What's going on, Officer White?" Curtis asked. He was the oldest of the bunch and took on the role of spokesperson.

Before I could answer, or runaway and hide, Ted spoke up. "This here's a plugged-up septic tank, kids. This is what happens when adults don't take care of things. I am going to pump all this stuff out and into my truck."

"Cool! Can we watch?" Stacy asked, stepping closer to the tank.

Ted smiled at the children. "All right, all right, you can all watch, but stand back. This thing could suck-start a fighter jet."

Ted fired up the pump motor, which had the horsepower of a battleship, and thrust the hose down into my tank. A great swirling occurred in the black water and the motor groaned with the burden.

"Here she goes, kids!" Ted shouted.

"Cool," said Samantha. "Look at all the little floaters being sucked under."

By this time Ken had come home for lunch and took an observation post behind Ashley, who was holding her nose and grinning widely. I wanted desperately to go inside and hide, but felt I should stay for the process, unsure of the proper etiquette required for such a procedure. Besides, although it was extremely embarrassing and humiliating, my family and me were the very source of the neighborhood entertainment.

"We're down to the solids now," Ted announced, reaching over and directing the hose to the bottom of the tank. "Watch the hose jump when I suck up this stuff," he said, moving the black pipe with uncalled-for dramatics.

Ken put his arm around my shoulder and gave me a brotherly hug. "This is just one part of the joys of home ownership."

Ted leaned over and was nearly inside the tank for the final cleaning process. He cleaned each nook and cranny, making sure all remnants were gone before pulling the hose away and shutting off the auxiliary pump. The kids got on their bikes and sped away, no doubt looking for others who did not have the opportunity to witness the event. Ted watched them travel down my road then pulled out a pad of paper and began making out the bill.

Ted told me the price, which was far less than I expected, and looked at my torn-up yard and the now empty tank. "Have me come out once a year or so," he said, taking my check and shaking my hand.

Minutes later I was left standing next to what used to be a fairly nice yard, with Ken, who was still grinning.

"There are many advantages to living in the country," he said. "Unfortunately, this is not one of them."

Ken walked back across the road and entered his house with a polite wave. My wife greeted me when I came up the stairs with the receipt.

"I guess we could call this flush with pride day," she said.

THE POWER OF RIVERS

THE KENAI RIVER IS GREEN. IT'S NOT GREEN LIKE A WELL-KEPT lawn or maple leaves or even Kermit the Frog, but it really is green. The water looks like mint mouthwash poured from a giant bottle, a translucent color that makes you wonder how it happened. And it's a big river with a powerful current that may not roar, but moans with a deep strength. Watching the Kenai is like being near a great green artery of a living planet.

Each river, no matter how large or small, possesses something special that it holds within its banks. In the Kenai, it's salmon. I don't mean the smallish washed-out salmon that lay in chain grocery store display cases or in small cans with colorful labels. I mean real salmon. The salmon of the Pacific feature a color and size found nowhere else on earth. This river is home to bold salmon and each year countless thousands of them return to their birthplace to spawn. Fishermen from around the globe come to fish this rich fishery.

My drive to the Kenai was a pilgrimage of sorts. I had been away from Alaska for eight years and had returned for a promotional book tour for *Alaska Behind Blue Eyes*. Twelve cities in sixteen days was a schedule that turned me from an otherwise calm person to something best described as wired. Following a highly promoted signing in an Anchorage Borders bookstore, I headed down to my next stop, the city of Kenai. Here I found myself with an entire evening off from the book signing circuit. This break from the exhausting tour made me feel almost guilty as I drove slowly toward the river. I did not come to fish, although to some who know me that may seem strange. Because of the hectic tour schedule, I brought no salmon equipment. My reason for this pilgrimage was just to be near the river. I needed a river on this night. I longed for its calmness.

It was not a long walk down to the Kenai. A wide and heavily used path from the parking area winded slowly downhill before ending at the gravel bank. I call it gravel, but actually the Kenai is lined with stones. Big stones. The kind of stones that farmers pick from their fields. Stones that homeowners use for fireplaces. The strong and ever rising and falling current does not allow for stones smaller than a grapefruit. On each side of the river the flat banks were nearly one hundred feet wide. I found this spot eight years before at a time when I was single and free and could take trips to grand rivers for no reason other than to fish and think. I did a lot of both back then.

A few people stood waist deep in the green water, casting spin-n-glow plugs in the deep run. Overhead the sun was settling to a deep yellow as it sank toward the spruce on the opposite bank. Sea gulls floated up and down the current waiting for fish scraps. Every few minutes someone would yell, "Fish on" and everyone would move away until the salmon was flopping on the stones. I found the same dead spruce log close to the water that eight years ago was one of my thinking places. The smooth gray wood was still sturdy as I sat and enjoyed the lowering sun and the salmon fighting against the rods in the green water.

I enjoyed watching the fishermen, but it was one young boy who drew my interest. He was about eight, give or take a year or two, and stood in the shallow water with more determination than I have ever seen. He was wearing hip boots that were several sizes too large and his legs were stuffed into them with garbage bags for extra protection from the cold water. An equally large rain slicker covered his body, almost to the boots. In his hand was a giant heavy salmon rod with a shiny spoon. Because of his size, and the watchful eyes of his parents, he could not wade very far into the water. He had found a quiet area away from the other fisherman and near my log where he intently cast over and over again into the mint-green water. His father and mother sat on some large stones near me and watched him. Each time the spoon drifted through the current the boy looked hopeful, as if each cast would bring a giant salmon. Every once in a while he would look back toward mom and dad, seeking their approval and also with the look that he did not wish to leave anytime soon. I smiled constantly while watching him and remembered my early days of fishing while my parents looked on. But something was different. Something was wrong with this family. I could feel it.

The boy's parents would smile when their son looked at them, but their faces changed when he went back to fishing. Mom and dad talked quietly with sad faces, watching their boy try for a salmon. The man tossed a small rock a few feet and rubbed his hands together while his wife crossed her arms and looked at the setting sun and the impossibly green water flowing by. The boy was oblivious to their deep thoughts and continued casting, running back and forth in front of them, grinning and knowing that the next attempt would connect him with a great fish.

For over an hour I watched the boy fish, and his parents become more and more depressed. I had to know what was happening. This, of course, was none of my business. I knew that, but I would not be able to leave without knowing more. I rose from my old log and walked to the father's side, and sat on a large stone next to him. I picked up a piece of driftwood and tapped it nervously against a rock. "Should have brought my rod," I said, looking to a man downstream who was fighting a rather large salmon. "Lot of fish in the river right now." The man looked downstream, following my eyes and said nothing. He took out a cigarette and tapped it on his leg before searching for a lighter. In front of us his boy inched several feet upstream and cast again into the swirling water. He looked at the boy and smiled. His grin caused his mother, who was standing a couple feet away, to smile back. "Sure is a nice evening for fishing," I offered, hoping for some reaction.

The man took a long drag on his cigarette and looked again at his son. "Yeah," he said quietly.

"I've been watching your boy fish," I said. "I'll tell you what, give that kid a few years and he will be up to his waist in water and landing the big ones."

The mother looked at me quickly with a horrified expression and walked away toward her son. She stood next to the current and ran her fingers through her hair, watching the lowering sun gently touch the spruce tree. The man tapped his cigarette against his rock and took another long drag, holding the smoke deep within his lungs. He looked at me and then at his son wading in the shallow water.

"My son is dying," he said slowly.

Inside my chest my heart throbbed with pain as a wash of instant sadness flowed through my body. "I'm sorry. I didn't mean to . . . "

"You didn't know," he said, taking another puff and looking at his wife standing next to the green water. "You'd never know it by watching him, would you?" The man forced a slight smile and watched his son make another cast.

"Look, sir, I had no idea . . ."

"He starts chemotherapy in the morning. Up in Anchorage. His doctor says it may give him a few more months. Or the treatment may kill him. Bobby knows that he is sick. Not how sick, but sick enough that he will be in the hospital for a long time. Bobby wanted to go fishing once more before tomorrow."

I wanted to say something. Really, I did. After all I am a writer and someone who cares for people who suffer. But here I was, sitting along one of the great rivers with people in pain near me and I could think of nothing to say. Across the Kenai, the sun was beyond the spruce, sending golden shards across the hopelessly green water and onto a small boy wishing for salmon, and fighting for his life. The man smashed out his cigarette against the rock and followed the sun to his boy. I prayed for God to give the kid one salmon. If I could have, I would have jumped into the green water and brought one to him. Suddenly the man jumped up.

"That's it Bobby," he shouted, running across the large stones to his son. The boy held the rod over his head and tried to reel in, but the salmon was too strong. With his father's encouragement the boy followed the fish downstream, away from my log and into deeper water.

"Keep your rod tip up!" his father yelled. He followed his son closely, not touching him but staying within a few feet. Beyond them, in the deep pool, the salmon rolled twice, cutting back upstream and into the stronger current. The boy stopped, unable to go further. His father held his shoulders, shouting words of encouragement, but not taking the rod. The sun turned the green river to gold as the salmon jumped three times, then weakened, coming toward the bank. It skidded on the large stones and flopped at the boy's feet. The man took the fish behind the gills and held it up high, patting his son on the shoulder and looking toward his wife who was smiling with tears in her eyes.

The boy took the fish and held it like a baby in his arms, becoming covered in slime and scales. He walked toward his mother while his father followed with the large rod. They met near my old log. I could not hear what they were saying.

Turning away, I walked downstream where there were no fishermen and watched the darkening green water. An eagle soared over the river, its wingtips nearly touching the water. In front of me the current surged with power. In a quiet pool next to the shore, a male salmon lay on its side, covered with white fungus and finned slowly. I watched him for a long time before reaching in and pushing him back into the green powerful river.

STANDING GROUND

MARK GRABBED A SPRUCE LIMB AND PULLED HIMSELF ONE STEP
higher on the rocks. Leaning forward, he jumped ahead
several steps before stopping on a rare flat section of the
trail. He backed up to another large spruce so his pack would have
some support and looked at the blue sky dotted with large fluffy
clouds, which were barely visible under the tangled treetops. I struggled over the rocks and took several awkward steps before stopping
nearby.

Our labored breathing was the only sound as we rested. I looked
up at the trail where it continued over the sharp rocks and zigzagged
up the mountainside. It had been more than two hours of hard
climbing, and we had yet to reach the halfway point. Mark swatted
at the cloud of insects hovering over his head and looked at me with
concern.

"Say, Al, please tell me again why we are making this hike. With
all this pain I feel it is important to clarify the reason that we are on
a mountainside, in almost one hundred percent humidity, abusing
our nearly middle-aged bodies." Mark shifted his pack and winced
at the pain. "I mean, what if we're killed? I want my loved ones to
know we died for a good cause."

"I've told you at least fifteen times! I told you about this hike before we left Michigan. We talked about it on the flight to Alaska. We discussed it this morning!"

"I know, I know, it's just that I want to hear it again. For the last two hours I've had a lot of time to think about this mission. By the way, what are the long-term effects of dehydration?"

I smiled at my friend and pulled the water bottle from my pack, tossing it playfully to him. "Okay," I said, watching as he took a long pull from the bottle. "We are climbing to the summit of Dewey Mountain to take the cover shot for my new book. Well, near the summit anyway. Like I said before, there's this rocky ridge where . . ."

"Look, Al," Mark said quickly, taking another drag from the bottle and replacing the cap. "*Alaska Behind Blue Eyes* was successful. Couldn't you have hired a couple of college kids who love nothing more than to assault a peaceful mountain? You know, guys with long legs, strong backs, good hair and teeth? Kids with names like Ryan or Skip. Guys that wear a lot of purple and teal-green. Yeah, this would be an easy jaunt for a Skip. I can see him with a pair expensive sunglasses hanging from a bright yellow cord, playfully *jogging* up this trail. I'll bet he would . . ."

"It's not the same!" I shot back. "I know exactly where the photo has to be taken."

"Okay, then, how about a helicopter?"

"Terrain's too rough to land."

Mark looked at me with his best sarcastic expression as he threw back the water bottle. "Oh good, I was hoping it would be rough."

"Besides, I *need* to do this."

"I knew there was something more!" Mark shouted. "Okay, out with it. I'm opening up lung tissue that I haven't used since the back-seat of a 1975 Pontiac, and I have a right to know!"

"It's my standing ground," I said, quietly.

Mark took a paper towel from his pocket and wiped his forehead. He glanced up at the rocky trail and then returned the carefully folded towel to his pocket. "Your *what?*" he asked, lowering his eyebrows to confrontation level.

"My *standing ground*. Remember when you were a kid and you had a special place. It might have been a fort you made with your friends, or a certain tree you climbed, or a rock you sat on, but it was all yours and you went there to think things over. You went there not because it was special to anyone else, but just special to you. This mountain ridge is my place. You don't take a helicopter to a standing ground. You don't hire restless college students to tell you about it. You get there by your own will."

"Okay, I'll stop complaining for awhile. Let's get going toward your promise land. By the way, I don't suppose you have one *closer* to town . . . do you?"

I laughed and playfully slugged my friend's shoulder as I hiked past. Mark moved from the tree and followed grudgingly behind as I began climbing the next steep section of the trail. Sharp black and gray granite jutted from the narrow path, like the teeth of a monster, making each step carefully planned.

Great branches from the giant spruce hung down to the trail like opened hands that guided us with prickly fingers. Tall ferns and devil's club plants shielded the trail from sunlight, keeping the rocky ground moist with the morning dew. All around the thick air hung like an invisible blanket, soft and comforting, but at the same time draining our energy. It seemed like each step was filled with effort to gain ground from the mountain. The trail cut against the mountain in forty-five degree angles for a hundred feet or more, then switched back to the other direction. Because of the steepness, a straight trail would be impossible to follow. With each step I could feel a sharp pain in my legs as tired muscles worked against the force of gravity.

My stop in Skagway, Alaska, was the midway point in a tightly regimented book promotional tour. Just two months before I had released *Alaska Behind Blue Eyes*, a collection of stories and essays based on my experiences as a police officer in Skagway. What began as a hobby and a lifelong dream of being an author had turned into a nearly full-time job of book marketer. Sales of the two-hundred-forty page collection surpassed my wildest expectations and resulted in a national distribution contract. Before I could fully grasp the impact of my first book, I was on a plane to start a fourteen-day, sixteen-city tour of the Alaska I had left behind eight years before. I had arranged for several appearances in Skagway, leaving time, of course, to fish for my beloved grayling and for the hike up Dewey Mountain.

Mark, being the good friend he is, volunteered to accompany me on this venture as personal assistant, first-time book cover photographer, and fishing buddy.

After about a half-hour I looked back at Mark struggling up the trail. He had found a dead spruce branch and had fashioned a walking staff to aid his climbing. At some point he donned a red bandanna that hung over his head and neck, no doubt to protect his flesh from the swarming gnats. I stopped at a switchback and watched as he approached.

"Hey Mark!" I yelled. "You look like a woodland shepherd!"

Mark climbed the last few steps to my resting-place, breathing deeply in the heavy air. He leaned against a rock outcrop and looked up at the seemingly never-ending trail.

"Listen," he said suddenly. In the distance I could hear the sound of falling water.

"We're at the halfway point. That's the Storybook River."

"The *Storybook* River?" he asked, still looking up the trail. "Is that your name or Alaska's name?" Mark was used to my habit of assigning my own titles to special places.

"My name, of course. Come on, I'll show you something wonderful."

I moved ahead over the next steep section, pushing myself over the rocks and fallen limbs. The trail leveled out slightly as I approached the river. It had been eight years since I felt the rushing water against my hands. Mark came up behind me as I walked off the trail and into the deep forest. It was difficult to squeeze through the spruce limbs and underbrush outside the trail. A sharp wall of fern-covered shale shot out against the slope like a warning, making us move gingerly along its base. Beyond the wall, the forest opened somewhat. A thick carpet of bright-green moss covered the forest floor and was saturated with the river's mist. I walked slowly to a giant boulder that rose from the moss like an icon and took off my pack to look at the river.

"My God," Mark said. He stopped beside the gray boulder and took off his pack. He kneeled by the water and dipped his hand into the strong, ice-cold current. "It's like something out of a fairytale. If this isn't a standing ground, I don't know what is," he said following the river with his eyes.

"Wonderful, isn't it?" I said, watching my friend discover the miracles of Southeast Alaska. I sat back against the boulder and felt the cool mist cover my face.

The Storybook River is created high in the upper Dewey Mountains by an ancient glacier. Most of the glacier water runs to Upper Lake and then down the mountainside in a cascade before reaching the ocean. Some of the water, however, flows along this trail destined for the Skagway River. What makes the Storybook unique is that flows unlike any other river I have seen. Water always takes the path of least resistance, carving out the earth beneath and making a streambed. This bed moves over time, creating distinct channels and a change of vegetation growth. In Michigan, and most other areas, rivers are lined with banks of thick brush. Rivers, as a rule, do not flow through forests without making a change in surrounding vegetation. The Storybook is different. The river runs down through the forest in a narrow channel, held in by the surrounding rock. There are no brushy banks, only a moss-covered forest floor and towering spruce trees. Although it flows down a steep mountain, the flow is not as rapid as one would think. The Storybook follows the natural switchbacks and becomes riffles and pools as it travels downward. Nowhere on the planet have I ever seen a river that flows so unobstructed and magically.

Mark stood and walked along the river, pausing at a shallow pool. "Tell me that's gold," he said.

I smiled, remembering that particular pool and my first reaction to seeing the shimmering flakes in the soft gravel. "Okay, that's gold. Why don't you pick up a hat full and we won't have to work for a couple years?"

Mark kneeled down and scooped some flakes from the pool. "Iron pyrite?" he asked, rubbing the tiny fragments between his fingers.

"You got it buddy. Fool's gold. Funny that you were so quick to find such a rich deposit." I laughed and knelt beside him, looking over the pool. The water was gin-clear and flowed over the gravel bed softly before tumbling down the mountain and creating yet another pool. Mixed in with the gravel was a light dusting of the pyrite.

"You know, Al, this would make a great cover for your new book. I could take your picture next to the river," Mark said.

"Not the same, bud. You will understand when we get to the top. This is a great place, though. Sometimes I would start the hike and stop here to rest, only to spend so much time here that I turned around and went back to town."

"I don't suppose there is any chance of that happening today?"

"Not a chance, Mark. Not today. Come on, we need the afternoon light for the shot."

We went back to the trail and started climbing. The trail now went through the steepest part of the mountain, with only fifty feet or less between switchbacks. At times we would climb for a half-hour, only to look back and see that only several hundred feet of elevation had been gained. As we climbed, the forest thickened, leaving only spruce that were tightly packed on the rocky ground.

Two hours later we climbed among stunted-looking trees. The tallest were now barely ten feet high and had a twisted look, like giant banzai projects. "We're almost there," I shouted back at Mark. "See how small the spruce are? We're getting near the tree line."

Mark reacted to my observation by tripping on a rather large piece of shale and falling sideways into a spruce trunk. "Oh, good!" he shouted, dusting off dead needles and kicking at the offending obstacle. "Soon we will only have to deal with the jagged rocks. Lucky for me that hard tree limb broke my fall. I may have landed on the soft moss."

"It gets better from here."

"Compared to what?" Mark asked, bringing out his best cynical voice.

At this level the forest began to open, leaving only a rocky trail that wandered like a gray snake up the mountain. On each side wild-flowers bloomed in little pockets where they could root in the thin soil. With each curve of the trail the trees grew smaller and slightly more yellow due to the poor soil quality. Before long, they opened to small groups surrounded by yellow-green grass. Ahead the twin Dewey peaks loomed above the remaining trees. Within minutes I could see the lake.

Resting beyond a rolling mountain meadow, filled with white and yellow wildflowers lay Upper Lake. Only a sliver was visible, but the pale-blue water shimmered in the sunlight and made me wonder why I ever left this majestic land. Mark walked to my side and looked ahead as more of the lake came into view with each step. Behind the lake the twin peaks loomed like guardians to one of Alaska's most precious jewels. When the entire lake was visible, we stopped and looked over the valley.

"It's like we're in God's amphitheater," Mark said quietly. He took off his pack and reached for his camera, then paused. "I've never seen anything like this. How could you ever leave Alaska?"

I said nothing and followed Mark's eyes across the valley. The small lake was the color of a young girl's eyes, satin-blue with a deep indigo center. Being above the tree line, the banks were covered in white stones that ringed the lake like a dainty necklace before blending in with the rich, long grass. On the far side of the lake the smaller peaks that connected the twin Dewey Mountains formed a semicircle with giant gray walls dusted on the top with snow. Mark took several photos and then stopped, looking at me.

"Film cannot possibly capture the wonder of this place," he said. "You certainly know how to pick a standing ground."

"We're not there yet," I said, watching his expression.

"What could possibly make a better cover than this place?"

"Up there," I said, pointing to the right, toward a high rocky ridge.

"That's another two thousand feet!"

"More or less."

"And *up there*, is better than *down here*?"

"Yes."

Mark shook his head and began walking toward the ridge. He looked back and smiled. "You know, Al, I am beginning to believe that it is."

The rocky ridge that I pointed to was just that; a ridge consisting of nothing but rocks and boulders, some larger than cars. It was created when, because of some natural event, a large section of the

South Dewey peak fell down the mountainside. What remained was a treacherous collection of gray granite and shale that had been at rest for a million years, give or take a few. Compared to the forest trail Mark and I had just climbed, our hike to the ridge top was, to say the least, stressful. We would step from boulder to boulder, constantly looking ahead for the next passable section of rock. At times we would hit a dead-end and have to retrace our steps to try another route. Compounding the difficulty was the fact that each step was an effort to retain traction on the steep climb. Two hours later we were near the top.

Here we climbed easily. The rocks on this section were relatively small and filled in with yellow-green lichens, making for a nearly pleasant climb. I picked up my pace and moved away from Mark, looking at the highest point. Minutes later I stood on my standing ground. A strong breeze came up from the valley, swirling around us and cooling our sweat-soaked clothing. The once mostly blue sky had darkened to various shades of gray that pressed down on us. Some of the clouds drifted by, just over our heads. Mark made his way to my side and looked out at something magnificent.

In front of us the ground fell away in a cascade of ancient rock. Below that, the deep green of the forest loomed dark and foreboding. Further down lay the pristine fiord of the North Pacific Ocean, turquoise green and flecked with silver light. Across the sea, the opposing mountains exploded from the water, lush and forested at the base and capped with silver-gray granite and bright snow. From the snow line came the glaciers.

From this very spot, twenty-seven glaciers could be seen without optical aids. They crawled downward toward the trees like mouthwash-blue growths, shining brightly with raw power. Below them came the waterfalls. Giant cascades of angry water rode the mountain toward the sea beneath each glacier. Even from over two miles away, their raw power could be heard from this lofty stand.

After eight years, I was finely back on my standing ground.

Mark stood silently, looking out over a view few would ever see. He began to speak, then stopped and shrugged his shoulders, possibly saying more with his actions than his words ever could. I walked away from my friend and sat on the lichen-covered ground. After several minutes he came to my side with his camera and several rolls of film.

"Before we begin, how about we sit for awhile? For some reason I need to quiet right now," he said distantly, looking out over Alaska.

I breathed deeply; smelling the salty odor of the ocean mixed with old forests and timeworn mountains. Eight years of memories came flooding back, of a time when I was younger and could capture life's adventure in a single trip to a grand place. I sat by my friend's side and tossed a stone toward the forest.

After several minutes Mark stood and looked at me. "Come on," he said. "I want to take a picture of you and your standing ground."

Additional Information

If you would like to purchase autographed soft cover copies of *Standing Ground* and/or *Alaska Behind Blue Eyes*, you may send $14.95 per copy, plus $4.00 for shipping and handling, to:

Dark River
P.O. Box 436
Clare, MI 48617

If you would like to contact the author, you may write to him at the above address or e-mail him at:
alanwhite48617@yahoo.com